PORTRAIT OF S. ALBANS CATHEDRAL

PUBLISHER'S NOTE

THIS in one of a series of books called THE ENGLISH CATHEDRALS. In each of its volumes the author has sketched, authoritatively, the history and the physical features of one cathedral. To this text has been added a range of photographs showing the architecture, as a whole and in detail. These pictures exemplify the advances made in the technique of photography in recent years, and are indeed the main feature of the series. Together, the text and pictures form a more complete 'portrait' than is elsewhere available in book form.

The book is so arranged as to inform the home reader and to guide the actual visitor, for whom an itinerary is given on PLAN facing page 9.

Titles in this Series

DURHAM*	WELLS
CANTERBURY*	YORK
SALISBURY*	ELY
LINCOLN*	EXETER
S. ALBANS*	NORWICH
GLOUCESTER	WINCHESTER

Already published

S. ALBANS ABBEY FROM THE LAKE

THE ENGLISH CATHEDRALS

Portrait of
S. ALBANS
CATHEDRAL

G · H · COOK

AUTHOR OF
Mediaeval Chantries and Chantry Chapels

PHOENIX HOUSE
London

FOREWORD

As a 'Portrait of S. Albans Cathedral' the following pages treat of the forms and lineaments that compose the whole, moulded by the religious and architectural ideals of the Middle Ages. To appreciate the cathedral as a piece of mediaeval architecture, one should know something of the purposes it served, of the historic influences which left their impress on the fabric and of the builders and craftsmen who here expressed the aspirations of their time in material form. By such approaches, it is hoped, will an understanding of the cathedral be arrived at.

S. Albans is a cathedral of the Modern Foundation. The abbey church might well have been made the cathedral of a new diocese when the monastery was suppressed in 1539. Henry VIII had drawn up in his own handwriting a list of thirteen 'bishoprics to be new made', including S. Albans, but in the end only six new sees were created, and, the claims of S. Albans being ig-nored, the abbey church became parochial and remained so until late in the nineteenth century.

Architecturally its importance rests on the Early Norman work in the nave, transepts and central tower, and in the lay-out of the eastern arm, which may be regarded as the perfect English method of planning a great monastic church that was the resort of pilgrims from far and wide.

The Post-Reformation history of the abbey is one of centuries of neglect and ill-usage. The alterations made in the fabric in the nineteenth century by Sir Edmund Beckett, later Lord Grimthorpe, involved the destruction of much that should have been preserved; from end to end of the cathedral the stones bear witness to the damage wrought by this headstrong and over-bearing spoiler who 'with the power of a bottomless purse carried everything before him' during the twenty years the building was entrusted to his care.

Made in 1951 in Great Britain
Set and printed at Plymouth by Latimer, Trend & Co., Ltd. for
PHOENIX HOUSE LIMITED
38 William IV Street London W.C.2

First published 1951

CONTENTS

ILLUSTRATIONS

ACKNOWLEDGMENTS

The author and publisher wish to acknowledge their indebtedness to the following photographers for the illustrations in this book:

Aero-Pictorial Ltd., 3
Mrs Becknell, 9
Gerald Cobb, 69
Country Life Ltd., 33
Fred H. Crossley, 11, 15, 19, 22, 23, 27, 29, 38, 44, 57, 62, 66
Herbert Felton, 5, 28, 35, 64, 70

E. C. le Grice, 4
National Buildings Record, 6, 7, 8, 12, 14, 16, 17, 25, 26, 30, 36, 37, 39, 43, 49, 52, 53, 54, 55, 56, 59, 60, 65
C. H. Noble, 20, 67
Photochrom Co. Ltd., 40, 50
Photo-Precision Ltd., 1, 24, 46, 47, 51
John H. Stone, 32, 41, 42, 63, 68
Rev. F. R. P. Sumner, 2, 10, 13, 18, 31, 45, 48, 58, 61
E. W. Tattersall, 21

PLAN OF
S. ALBANS CATHEDRAL

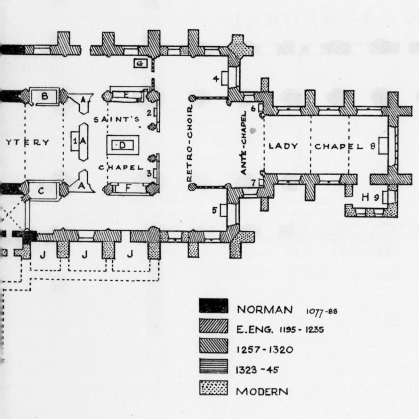

NORMAN 1077-88

E.ENG. 1195-1235

1257-1320

1323-45

MODERN

AL

...rine of S. Alban; E. Watching House;

...Transfiguration; J. Chapels (destroyed);

...n.

...Tapers; 6. S. Edmund; 7. S. Peter; 8. Our Lady;

...dy; 15. S. Thomas of Canterbury; 16. S. Benedict;

...pillar; 21. S. Katherine; 22. S. Andrew; 23. Our Lady

BUILDING SEQUENCE

THE FOLLOWING SUMMARY GIVES IN brief the building sequence of the main parts of the cathedral.

1077–1088. The central tower, the transepts and parts of the nave, of Abbot Paul's Norman church.

1195–1235. Four western bays of the nave and portions of the three porches in the west front.

1257–1320. The presbytery, Saint's chapel and the retrochoir (much restored).

c. 1325. Completion of the Lady Chapel.

1323–1345. Five bays of the south nave arcade and the adjoining aisle.

c. 1363. The rood-screen.

c. 1400. The timber watching-house in the Saint's chapel.

1420. Chapel of the Transfiguration (rebuilt).

1445. Chantry chapel of Humphrey, Duke of Gloucester.

1480–1484. The Wallingford altar-screen.

c. 1510. Chantry chapel of Abbot Ramryge.

1856–1878. Gilbert Scott's restorations; Lord Grimthorpe's restoration of west front and sundry other alterations.

AN ITINERARY FOR VISITORS

THE VISITOR TO S. ALBANS CATHEDRAL is advised to examine the several parts of the interior according to their building sequence and so trace the successive stages by which the church attained its present form. The tour should commence beneath the central tower and after seeing the transepts, the visitor should pass into the ritual choir west of the crossing. By way of the south aisle he should then enter the nave where the Norman bays on the north side will claim his attention and farther west the thirteenth-century extension of the nave. Retracing his steps eastwards the visitor can compare the Decorated bays on the south side with those to the west and after examining the rood-screen he should make his way by the south aisle into the presbytery where the altar-screen and Abbot Ramryge's chantry chapel are seen to perfection. The Saint's chapel beyond, with the shrine and watching-house is then entered from the south choir aisle, after which the visitor should proceed farther east into the retrochoir and the Lady Chapel, returning by the north choir aisle.

Externally the central tower, the cloister-arcading on the wall of the south aisle, the west front and the great gatehouse are features of interest that none should fail to see.

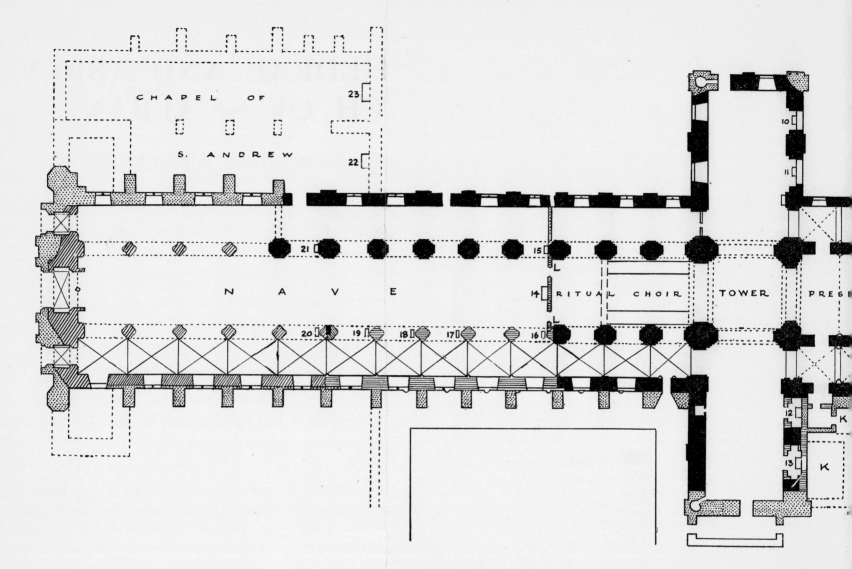

PLAN OF S. ALBANS CATHEDR

A. *Wallingford Screen;* B. *Ramryge Chapel;* C. *Wallingford Chapel;* D. *Sh*
F. *Duke Humphrey's Chapel;* G. *Shrine of S. Amphibalus;* H. *Chapel of the*
K. *Vestries (destroyed);* L. *Rood Scree.*

SITES OF THE MEDIAEVAL ALTARS

1. *High Altar;* 2. *S. Hugh;* 3. *The Salutation;* 4. *S. Michael and S. Katherine;* 5. *Our Lady of the Fou*
9. *S. Saviour;* 10. *Holy Trinity;* 11. *S. Osyth;* 12. *S. John Evangelist;* 13. *S. Stephen;* 14. *Our La*
17. *Our Lady, removed to 14;* 18. *S. Benedict, removed to 16;* 19. *S. Thomas, removed to 15;* 20. *Our Lady of the*

THE CATHEDRAL AND ABBEY CHURCH OF S. ALBAN

'In Britain's isle was holy Alban born'

Origin of the Cathedral · The Story of S. Alban · Foundation of the Abbey by King Offa II · The premier Benedictine monastery in England · Pilgrimages to the Shrines of S. Alban and S. Amphibalus · Monastic hospitality · The pre-Conquest and Norman abbeys · Abbot Paul's church and what remains to-day · The Relics of S. Alban · The Early English West front and the extension of the Nave · Reconstruction of the Choir-arm in the thirteenth century · The Shrine of S. Alban · The Retrochoir and the Lady Chapel · The Calamity of 1323 and the Decorated bays of the Nave · The Rood-screen · The Watching-chamber in the Saint's Chapel · Abbot Wheathampstead · Humphrey Duke of Gloucester and his Chantry Chapel · Abbot Wallingford's Altar-screen · Chantry chapels, tombs and memorials in the Cathedral · The Abbey at the Reformation and since · Nineteenth-century restoration by Gilbert Scott · Elevation of the church to Cathedral rank in 1877 · Lord Grimthorpe's mutilations and innovations

ON THE LOW RISE opposite the site of the Roman city of Verulamium, the great church that is now the cathedral of S. Albans was reared in honour of the protomartyr of England and is said to mark the spot where he suffered death more than sixteen centuries ago. Over the grave of the martyr a little chapel was built, and from that humble beginning arose the vast pile that was elevated to the status of a cathedral in 1877. A monastery was founded on or near the site in 795 and for seven centuries and more, monks of the Benedictine order offered up prayer and praise in the abbey church sanctified as the resting-place of the remains of S. Alban. After the suppression of the monasteries by Henry VIII it served as a parish church for more than three centuries, until it was reconstituted as the cathedral church of a new diocese that was carved out of Rochester seventy-three years ago.

The story of S. Alban which may or may not be legendary takes us back to the early years of the fourth century. During the Diocletian persecution, Albanus,

a Roman of good birth, living at Verulamium, sheltered a Christian priest named Amphibalus and himself embraced the faith. When search was made for Amphibalus, Albanus assisted him to escape and presented himself to the Roman soldiers, clad in the priest's garments. Haled before the magistrates, he refused to sacrifice to the Roman gods and was led forth to execution on the 'heading hill' across the Ver, the waters of which miraculously parted to permit passage. His protégé Amphibalus fled to Wales but was subsequently captured, brought to Verulamium and put to death at Redbourn a few miles away. When the persecution died out, a simple timber chapel described by Beda as 'of wonderful workmanship' was built over the burial place of Albanus at a spot known as Holmhurst on the summit of a hill north of Verulamium. It was, however, swept away during the Saxon invasions of the sixth century and for the next two hundred years the grave of the martyr was forgotten.

FOUNDATION OF THE ABBEY

According to Matthew Paris, S. Albans abbey was founded as an act of expiation by Offa II, King of Mercia, for the murder of Ethelbert, King of East Anglia. Offa had invited Ethelbert to his court on the pretence of bestowing the hand of his daughter upon him, but the prospective son-in-law was put to death instead. In 793 when Offa was at Bath, an angel appeared to him in a vision and enjoined him to raise the body of Albanus out of the earth and deposit it in a worthy shrine. He related his vision to the Bishops of Lichfield, Lindsey, and Leicester, who with a crowd of followers of all ages made their way to Verulamium where they were met by the king, and with prayers and fasting, commenced the search for the martyr's remains. During the digging operations they were assisted by a light from heaven and eventually the grave was revealed by a ray of fire 'like the star that conducted the Magi to Bethlehem'. Amid the chanting of hymns the relics were conveyed in solemn procession to a little chapel outside Verulamium, and there Offa placed a circlet of gold round the skull of Albanus. In 795 the king resolved to build a monastery wherein the relics should be preserved, and journeying to Rome to obtain papal sanction, he induced Adrian I to canonize the first martyr of England. Special privileges were granted the Benedictine abbey thus founded. Peter's pence, a tax levied on Saxon landowners for the support of the Saxon college at Rome, was henceforward to be paid to the abbey of S. Albans; Offa and his sons heaped liberal benefactions upon the monastery, including the royal manor of Winslow, 60,000 acres of land in what is now the county of Hertfordshire and a tract of forest land in Middlesex. From the time of Offa's foundation there has been a church on the site of S. Albans cathedral. Around the abbey grew up a new town, the Roman city of Verulamium declined and in course of time was abandoned just as was Old Sarum when Salisbury cathedral was built in the thirteenth century.

As trustees of the relics of S. Alban, the abbots who ruled over the convent in the late tenth century lived in constant dread of Danish incursions. Vain was the hope that the abbey would escape the dire fate that befell monasteries in the path of the pagan destroyer. When Abbot Aelfric, 968–90, feared an in-

vasion, he concealed the relics of S. Alban in a wall and despatched a chest of other bones to the monastery of Ely, with a request for their safe custody. Believing them to be the true relics and loth to part with them when danger was past, the brethren at Ely substituted other bones in the chest which they duly returned. But they forthwith claimed that they alone possessed the remains of the saint. A century and a half later at the instance of Pope Adrian IV, three bishops held an inquiry and the monks of Ely under pain of excommunication were forced to admit that they had 'perpetrated sacrilege' and possessed none of the bones of S. Alban.

Throughout the Middle Ages S. Albans was the premier Benedictine establishment in this country. In the councils of the Church the abbot took precedence over all other abbots and further it was a mitred abbey. The conferring of the mitre, ring and gloves upon an abbot was a much-coveted distinction; as a spiritual lord he was entitled to a seat in Parliament. It was a proud moment for Abbot Robert of Gorham when he assumed the insignia for the first time at High Mass on Easter Sunday 1163. The same year at the Council of Tours, S. Albans was acknowledged to be the premier Benedictine abbey of England, a status contested by Westminster, which became a mitred abbey thirteen years afterwards.

Like many other Benedictine churches, S. Albans was famous as an object of pilgrimage. In so august a church, shrines and relics were indispensable. The main attractions were the shrines of S. Alban and S. Amphibalus, but there were lesser treasures upon which pilgrims could feast their eyes. In the time of Abbot Trumpington 1214–35, the convent acquired a much-valued relic, viz., a rib of S. Wulstan of Worcester and another prized treasure was a golden reliquary containing an arm of S. Jerome. A piece of the true Cross was presented to the abbey by a monk who brought it from Jehosaphat near Jerusalem. Relics were a profitable source of revenue to the convent, for the more the pilgrims were given to see the more liberal were their offerings.

The abbey was greatly favoured by royalty; kings and queens, the nobility and foreign potentates came hither to worship and make their gifts at the shrine of S. Alban. When Henry I visited the abbey in 1104 he granted the convent an annual fair of eight days

1 · THE TRANSEPTS AND CROSSING FROM THE SOUTH · Except for Lord Grimthorpe's circular window, the Norman transepts are largely in their original condition.

3 · AIR VIEW OF THE CATHEDRAL FROM THE SOUTH-WEST · The church has a total external length of 550 feet. At the crossing is the Norman tower of the eleventh century, and on the extreme left is the Great Gatehouse.

12

5 · THE CATHEDRAL FROM THE NORTH-WEST · To the left of the tower is the north transept which is said to occupy the site of S. Alban's martyrdom.

4 · THE TRANSEPTS AND CROSSING FROM THE NORTH-WEST · Beyond the great arches of the central tower is the south transept lighted by Lord Grimthorpe's Lancet windows.

6 · THE CATHEDRAL FROM THE EAST · In the foreground is the Lady Chapel with the little chapel of the Transfiguration on its left. Beyond the gable are the tower and the south transept.

7 · THE RITUAL CHOIR LOOKING WEST · The stalls now in the choir and the timber screen beyond are modern.

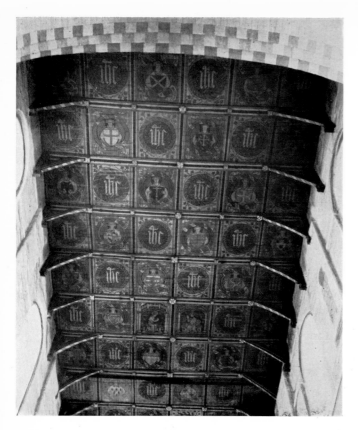

8 · THE ROOF OF THE RITUAL CHOIR · In the 66 panels of the timber ceiling are paintings of the sacred monogram alternating with heraldic shields of Edward III and his kinsfolk.

9 · THE CENTRAL TOWER · Built mainly of bricks from Verulamium, the tower, which is 144 feet high, was coated with plaster by the Norman builders.

10 · THE RITUAL CHOIR AND NORTH TRANSEPT FROM THE SOUTH-EAST · In the ritual choir which occupied part of the nave and the crossing were placed the monks' stalls. The pier in the centre is cut back to permit the fixing of the stalls.

15

11 · THE CENTRAL TOWER FROM BELOW · The wooden ceiling above the lantern stage is divided into panels, decorated with paintings of heraldic arms and the Red and White Roses. The paintings were applied in the sixteenth century. (*Left*)

12 · NORMAN TRIFORIUM IN THE NORTH TRANSEPT · The shafts, capitals, and bases, and the absence of ornament indicate work of the Early Norman period. (*Right*)

13 · NORMAN TRIFORIUM IN THE SOUTH TRANSEPT · Here the Norman builders re-used Saxon baluster-shafts, distinguished by the moulded rings. Above the sub-arches the plaster is stripped to show the Roman brickwork.

14 · NORMAN CLERESTORY IN THE NORTH TRANSEPT · In front of the round-arched windows is the clerestory way, a passage carried through the wall, for use when repairs to the fabric were necessary.

15 · NORMAN WALL-ARCADING IN THE SOUTH TRANSEPT · This late Norman arcading with intersecting arches and curious cotton-reel ornament, c. 1155–60, was originally in the slype outside the transept.

16 · THE PILGRIMS' DOOR · By this doorway in the north transept countless pilgrims entered the abbey church to visit the shrine of S. Alban. All the Roman brickwork was formerly coated with plaster.

18 · THE EAST WALL OF THE SOUTH TRANSEPT · The simple treatment is characteristic of Early Norman architecture. The two arches on the right formerly opened into apsidal chapels.

17 · THE SOUTH-WESTERN PIER AT THE CROSSING · The piers at the crossing are 43 feet in height and from them spring the arches of the central tower.

and conferred upon Abbot Daubeney the right to hold a court for minor offences committed within the liberty of S. Albans, a privilege that spelt trouble later. In 1115 Henry and Queen Matilda spent Christmas there and remained for the consecration of the Norman abbey. King John was at S. Albans the day after his coronation in May 1199, and between 1244 and 1259 Henry III was entertained by the abbot on seven occasions. After attending High Mass at the Feast of S. Thomas, 21 December 1244, he presented a rich pall and three golden bracelets to adorn S. Alban's shrine, and in 1257 at the Feast of S. Edward Confessor, he made gifts of costly silk hangings, bracelets and rings. Edward I presented a large image of silver-gilt to the shrine. After a visit to S. Albans in 1314, Edward II went on to Ely, and was there shown a shrine which the monks alleged contained the remains of S. Alban. Unconvinced, the king commanded it to be opened and when that was done, he pronounced that the authentic relics of the saint were at S. Albans. Edward the Black Prince was a frequent visitor; and when King John of France was brought captive to England after Poitiers 1356, he was foisted upon Abbot de la Mare for a time and was entertained in a manner befitting his state. Richard II presented a necklace to the image of the Virgin Mary in the Saint's chapel and on Ascension Day 1400 Henry IV attended High Mass in state.

After the first battle of S. Albans in 1455, Henry VI who had sought refuge in a baker's shop in the town was taken to the abbey as a prisoner-of-war; and on Shrove Tuesday 1461 he was there with Queen Margaret to return thanks at the High Altar for victory at the second battle of S. Albans and for the deliverance of his royal person. That same year immediately after the coronation of Edward IV Abbot Wheathampstead spent £85 on entertaining the youthful monarch and his entourage.

The demands made on conventual hospitality were so great that a new guest-house was built in the precincts in Abbot de la Mare's time for the accommodation of royal and noble visitors, especially for those who indulged in falconry and hunting, bringing in their train a small army of retainers. When Humphrey, Duke of Gloucester, a close friend of Abbot Wheathampstead, came with his lady to spend Christmas 1423 at S. Albans, he brought with him three hundred followers and stayed a fortnight. Hospitality on such a scale, a very broad interpretation of the Benedictine purpose, must have taxed the resources of the monastery to the utmost and the presence of boisterous and unruly retainers must have proved a disturbing element in the religious life of the convent.

As an architectural monument the cathedral is important in several respects. It is second only to Winchester cathedral in length, though less than two-thirds in superficial area; and its fully-developed layout, perfectly suited to its purposes, embodies the ideals of church-planning in the Middle Ages. The cathedral presents us with work of several phases of mediaeval architecture, from the Norman tower of the eleventh century to the Perpendicular chantry chapel of Abbot Ramryge. Amongst the notable features in the church are the reconstructed pedestal of S. Alban's shrine, the watching-house in the Saint's chapel, the rood-screen in the nave, and the glorious Wallingford screen that backs the High Altar.

On plan the cathedral is a cruciform building, with a nave thirteen bays long, flanked by north and south aisles; there are aisleless transepts, disproportionate in area to the rest of the church, and at the crossing rises a tower, 144 feet in height. The eastern limb, which is five bays long, embraces the presbytery and Saint's chapel, and beyond is a square retrochoir or ambulatory roofed at a lower level. At the extreme east is a rectangular Lady Chapel (see PLAN).

The internal length of the cathedral is about 520 ft.

The High Altar stands in the fourth bay of the presbytery east of the crossing and the lofty Wallingford altar-screen completely shuts off the Saint's chapel beyond. In monastic days the area at the crossing and the two eastern bays of the nave formed the ritual choir, where were the stalls occupied by the monks during their frequent services. This was the normal arrangement in Benedictine churches. The mediaeval stalls have long since disappeared, those now in the monks' choir dating from 1904. At the west end of the ritual choir, where the organ now is, stood a screen known as the pulpitum, and one bay farther west is the stone rood-screen, with two doorways for the passage of the double file of monks at procession times. Against the middle of the screen was the rood-altar.

From the twelfth century until the Reformation a parish chapel dedicated to S. Andrew was attached to the nave at the north-west (see PLAN).

The cathedral follows the natural slope (from east to west) of the ground on which it was built, and this accounts for the different floor levels that are reached by ascents at frequent intervals. At the western end of the nave is a rise of five steps and eight bays farther east three steps ascend to the level of the rood-screen. There is another step in the ritual choir and one more up to the crossing. Beneath the eastern arch of the tower, five steps lead up to the presbytery and another to the altar rails, beyond which four more reach the High Altar. Necessarily there are steps at several points in the aisles. The series of ascents from west to east elevated the pavement of the Lady Chapel about ten feet above that at the western end of the cathedral.

THE SAXON AND NORMAN CHURCHES

Of the pre-Conquest abbey church little or nothing is known. Preparations for an entire rebuilding of the Saxon church with Roman bricks, stone and rubble from Verulamium were made by Abbots Ealdred and Eadmer in the first half of the eleventh century but came to nought, and save for a few baluster-shafts in the transepts nothing remains of the Saxon period in the fabric of the cathedral now standing.

At S. Albans as elsewhere the Conquest wrought tremendous changes; almost without exception the Norman ecclesiastics swept away the Saxon abbeys and churches which far from satisfied their ritualistic requirements. The last of the Saxon abbots, Frithrig or Frederic, 1066–77, a kinsman of King Cnut, put up a sturdy resistance to William of Normandy. By slow marches the Conqueror had passed the Thames at Wallingford and reached Berkhamsted, there to find that Abbot Frederic and his followers had felled trees to impede the invader. When the abbot together with Archbishop Aldred of York, Edgar Atheling and others met William at Berkhamsted, the Conqueror solemnly swore on the bones of S. Alban that he would keep inviolate the laws of the realm and be

'a loving lord' to them all. Notwithstanding, he seized lands between London and Barnet belonging to the abbey, some of which he conferred upon the rival abbey of Westminster. The disillusioned Frederic resigned office and retired to the monastery of Ely where he ended his days in 1077.

In June of the same year at the instigation of Lanfranc, Archbishop of Canterbury, the King appointed Paul, a Benedictine monk of Caen, to the vacant abbacy. Paul was a kinsman of the Archbishop; indeed rumour had it that he was Lanfranc's natural son. Be that as it may, the primate evinced a deep interest in the activities of the new abbot of S. Albans, who set himself a twofold task—to establish a monastic way of life in his house, that would be in keeping with the Norman ideal and to replace the Saxon abbey by a church comparable with those of Caen.

The Benedictine rule had been very laxly observed by the monks of pre-Conquest S. Albans; discipline was slack in such matters as food, dress and the rule of silence, and some of the abbots had been living there with their wives and families. The Norman, Paul, lost no time in reforming the convent and enforcing a strict compliance with the Rule, and by so doing earned S. Albans a reputation that brought it fame and importance. Scant respect was shown by the newcomer for his thirteen predecessors; he spoke of them as boors and blockheads, 'rudes et idiotas', and destroyed their tombs.

For the rebuilding of the abbey, towards which Lanfranc contributed 1,000 marks, Abbot Paul brought over from Normandy a band of masons, chief of whom was Master Robert, 'the most skilful mason in England'; so skilful indeed that the abbot presented him with the manor of Sarret, a gift the monks disapproved of, as the manor belonged to the convent. The Saxon abbey was speedily demolished and the site prepared for an imposing church, vaster in scale than Lanfranc's cathedral at Canterbury just completed. In 1088 after eleven years' work, the largest Norman church then in these islands, the nucleus of the present cathedral was completed. The most costly items in building were always stone and transport but the abbot and the masons at S. Albans were singularly fortunate. No need to import stone from Caen or to open up distant quarries, for close by lay the ruins of Verulamium, a quarry that furnished

Roman bricks and stone in abundance. Paul's masons ransacked the Roman remains and also made use of the stocks of timber, bricks and masonry, accumulated by Abbots Ealdred and Eadmer earlier in the century. Norman masons were nothing if not resourceful. The abbey was very largely built of Roman bricks coated with plaster, the bricks differing from those of to-day in size and measuring 17 in. by 8 in. by 2 in. and 11 in. by 6 in. by 2 in.

Modelled on the church of S. Stephen, Caen, Norman S. Albans exceeded it in dimensions, the total length being about 380 feet, i.e. nearly 100 feet greater than the Caen abbey.

On plan it consisted of an aisled nave of ten bays, a choir-arm four bays long, also aisled, north and south transepts each with two apsidal chapels at the east, and a tower at the crossing. The lay-out of the choir-arm terminating in three apses was the normal plan in both Normandy and England. The central apse in which stood the High Altar projected beyond the lateral apses and the choir was divided from its aisles by solid walls. Secondary altars were set up in the apses of the transepts and choir-aisles. A similar arrangement of apses in echelon was adopted about twenty years later in the planning of Binham Priory, Norfolk, a daughter house of S. Albans.

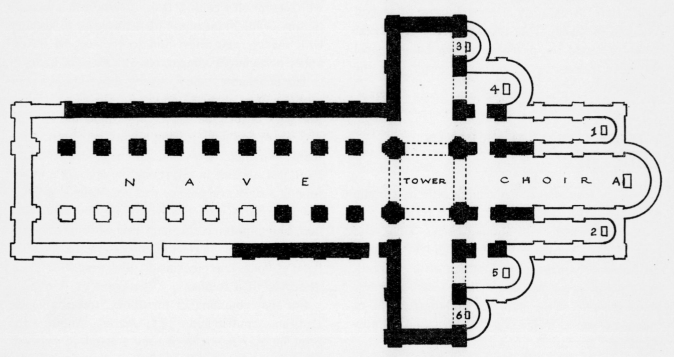

FIG. I. PLAN OF THE NORMAN ABBEY CHURCH, 1077–88
The parts that remain are in black
Altars: A, *High Altar*; 1, *Holy Innocents*; 2, *S. Nicholas and S. Blaise*; 3, *Holy Trinity*; 4, *S. Osyth*; 5, *Our Lady*; 6, *S. Stephen*

Though the abbey church was completed in 1088, five years before the death of Paul, it was not dedicated until the year 1115.

A lover of learning and described as '*eleganter litteratus*', Abbot Paul presented twenty-eight books to the house he had reformed and he built a scriptorium for monk-transcribers; thus laying the foundation of the foremost school of historians in mediaeval England. He also sent forth colonies of his monks to found daughter-houses at Belvoir (Lincs.),

Binham (Norfolk), Wallingford (Berks) and Hertford, and during his rule Tynemouth Priory (Northumberland) formerly a cell of Durham came into the possession of S. Albans.

The consecration of the abbey took place on Holy Innocents Day, 28 December 1115, during the abbacy of Richard Daubeney, 1097–1119, and the ceremony was performed by the Archbishop of Rouen in the presence of Henry I and Queen Matilda, the Bishops of Lincoln, Durham, Old Sarum and London and a great gathering of ecclesiastics and nobles. The king and queen were entertained by the abbot for eleven days. In recognition of the curing of his withered arm at the Translation of S. Cuthbert's relics at Durham in 1104, Abbot Daubeney built a chapel dedicated to S. Cuthbert on the east side of the cloistral buildings at S. Albans. The slab of Frosterley marble on a tomb in the south choir aisle of S. Albans is believed to be the mensa of the altar of S. Cuthbert and is marked with five consecration crosses. Soon after the consecration of Paul's abbey, S. Andrew's chapel at the north-west of the nave was built for parochial use.

REMAINS OF THE NORMAN ABBEY

Considerable portions of the Norman abbey remain to-day. The central tower, the most striking feature of the exterior has no equal in any Anglo-Norman church of the eleventh century and the piers which support it are impressive in the extreme. Despite the removal of the apsidal chapels and the unsightly alterations made in the nineteenth century, the transepts retain much of their Early Norman character. In the nave nine bays of the north arcade and three of the south are the work of Paul's masons, and portions of the solid walling dividing the choir from the aisles are of the same period.

The central tower, which is not quite square, being about eighteen inches less north to south than east to west, is built almost entirely of Roman bricks, the warm hue of which in a summer sun, is particularly pleasing. Originally the brickwork, in fact the whole of the Norman church inside and out was coated with plaster. Externally the tower is designed in three stages, lighted by round-arched windows and the angles are strengthened with flat pilaster-buttresses in the lower part and with circular turrets in the belfry stage. The huge piers at the crossing which carry the tower are 43 feet in height and the internal walls of the tower have galleries of three round arches with two sub-arches. Between the windows of the lantern stage are coloured heraldic shields of Edward I, Queen Eleanor, Richard Crouchback and Richard, Duke of Cornwall. The timber ceiling is divided into sixteen square panels, those in the centre displaying the arms of England, S. George, S. Alban and S.

Edward Confessor, around which are roundels of the Red and White roses. All the ceiling paintings date from the sixteenth century.

THE TRANSEPTS

The damage inflicted upon the transepts by Lord Grimthorpe was mainly confined to the end walls, that of the south transept being entirely rebuilt (p. 49). The Norman apsidal chapels had been swept away centuries before, and the arches that opened into them are now filled in with masonry. The two chapels in the south transept dedicated to Our Lady and S. Stephen were pulled down in the fourteenth century to make room for a treasury and vestries; and the chapels of Holy Trinity and S. Osyth in the north transept were demolished a century later but nothing was built in their place.

In the western corner of the north transept is the Norman doorway that was used by pilgrims who entered the abbey precincts by the Wax-House Gate at the north-east; and the recess in the western wall of the south transept, where are the bread-chests of Robert Skelton's bequest 1628, was originally a doorway opening into the east walk of the cloisters.

Of unique interest are the triforium openings high up in the eastern walls of the transepts, for the sub-arches spring from Saxon baluster-shafts that the Norman builders re-used. The shafts were turned in a lathe and are marked with rings at intervals, but the bases and cushion-capitals are Norman. In the spandrels of the triforium the Roman brickwork is laid bare.

The transepts were originally covered with timber roofs, which were replaced by flat ceilings in the fifteenth century, and these in turn have given place to modern high-pitched roofs.

The Norman bays of the nave, bold and plain, almost stark in character, must be the earliest in our greater churches. The nature of the material, brick and flint coated with plaster, precluded anything but the simplest architectural treatment; hence the massive square piers with recessed angles, the imposts that serve for capitals, and the square-edged orders or steps of the nave arches that correspond with the angles of the piers. Some attempt appears to have been made to provide two of the piers west of the rood-screen with cushion capitals but with little success. The bays are well defined by broad pilasters which rise the full height of the nave. The triforium which is about one-half the height of the nave arcade, consists of a single splayed arch in each bay, and a smaller round-arched window lights the clerestory. Except on bright days, the nave must have been very dark; so, to relieve the gloom, in the fifteenth century the roof of the north aisle was lowered beneath the triforium openings.

All the Norman architecture at S. Albans is devoid of carved ornament owing to the unsuitability of the material, but it may be argued that stone would have been equally free of ornament owing to the limited skill of the masons. It was not until well in the twelfth century that the Norman craftsman became an adept at carving ornament. The plaster of the walls and piers was lined in red to simulate banded courses of masonry, as can be seen on two piers west of the rood-screen. The sole enrichment employed to relieve the bareness of the dull plaster was colour, of which considerable traces still remain. The outer orders of the arches of the tower and nave are painted with alternating red and blue 'voussoirs' and on the soffits of the nave arches are chevron patternings of red and blue and other motifs like the star and lozenge.*

From Norman times there was everywhere the desire for additional altars in the greater churches. At S. Albans altars were set up against the western sides of the nave piers, an arrangement that involved little expenditure on the part of the convent. Though it is uncertain when these altars were first installed, early in the thirteenth century the walling above the altars was adorned with reredos paintings.

With such haste was the building of the Norman abbey pushed on, the chief concern being to see the big and imposing church completed, that the masons disregarded the essential need for sound foundations. Lord Grimthorpe discovered that the foundations of the piers were sufficiently large and strong but those of the aisle walls had been scamped. During a heavy thunderstorm in June 1936, whilst drainage was in progress outside the north wall of the nave, water entered the church through some holes that had been

dug there, and on examination it was found that the aisle-walls were standing on foundations only six inches deep, one of the many instances of the unsound methods of Norman builders in a hurry.

Both nave and aisles were roofed with timber, and probably the only vaulting in Paul's church was in the choir aisles, the western bays of which have groined vaults in plaster. The nave was covered with a flat ceiling like the lid-roof of Peterborough nave.

RELICS OF S. ALBAN

For more than three centuries the greatest treasure of the convent had been the remains of S. Alban. Nothing added to the sanctity and fame of a newly consecrated church more than a splendid shrine containing the bones of a local saint. So thought Abbot Geoffrey of Gorham, 1119–46. It chanced that amongst his flock was a monk-craftsman named Anketil, who in 1123 was entrusted with the task of making a new coffer or feretrum for the remains of S. Alban. From Matthew Paris we learn that Anketil had been goldsmith and master-of-the-mint to the King of Denmark before taking monastic vows at S. Albans. He was assisted by a lay-craftsman, Solomon of Ely, in making the feretrum, which was cased with plates of silver-gilt and studded with gems. When famine threatened the townspeople of S. Albans, Abbot Geoffrey, who had spent £60 on the feretrum, converted the gold and silver into money to relieve the distressed but eventually the coffer was remade and 'brought to great perfection both in ornament and magnificence'. However, a larger and more splendid shrine was fashioned during the rule of Abbot Simon, 1167–83. Anketil's coffer was enclosed within a new feretrum, designed and executed by 'Master John the goldsmith'. 'This laborious, sumptuous and most artistic work', wrote the chronicler, 'was placed in its present elevated position, that is, above the High Altar facing the celebrant, so that every priest offering mass may have both in sight and in heart the memory of the martyr.' The shrine was cased on two sides with embossed figures of gold and silver depicting the acts of S. Alban. At the east end was a large crucifix with Mary and S. John adorned with jewels and at the west was a *repoussé* panel of the Madonna enthroned and surrounded with gems. So costly was

---

* Chevron ornament carved in stone did not appear in Anglo-Norman architecture before *c.* 1110, an early instance occurring at Durham cathedral.

the feretrum that the convent had to resort to a Jewish moneylender, Aaron, to pay for it, and when finished it was so massive that it required four men to carry it.

In an age when the craze for relics of the saints obsessed bishops and abbots, the fame of S. Albans was still further enhanced by the acquisition of the remains of Amphibalus. Legendary though it may be, history repeated itself. In 1178 S. Alban appeared in a vision to a devout townsman and led him to the spot where Amphibalus lay buried at Redbourn, a few miles away, and when Abbot Simon was informed, the body was recovered. A procession of monks bearing with them the reliquary of S. Alban went forth to receive the remains which were given a temporary resting-place in the north aisle of the choir.

THE NEW WEST FRONT AND NAVE EXTENSION

For more than a century the Norman abbey church remained as Paul's masons had left it, but in the closing years of the twelfth century, under the rule of Abbot John de Cella, 1195–1214, alterations were begun at the west end of the church. Possibly the west front had become unsafe, or it may be that the abbot wanted a more dignified façade embracing twin towers and three deep porches. The work commenced with the building of a new façade thirty feet west of the old front and therefore involved lengthening the nave by three bays. Abbot John was badly served by the master-mason, Hugh de Godelif, 'an untrustworthy and deceitful man but a consummate craftsman'. By the time the foundations were in, the sum of 100 marks bequeathed by the abbot's predecessor had been squandered. The extravagance and dishonesty of Master Hugh and the lack of funds caused a complete stoppage of the work in the winter of 1197–8; the walls were but a few feet above ground and the masons with no prospect of receiving their pay downed tools and departed. Exposed to the wintry weather, the masonry was almost reduced to ruins and the state of the building excited the derision of the townspeople. In desperate need of money the abbot sent out some of the monks on a begging mission, accompanied by a young man who had been miraculously restored to life at S. Alban's shrine.

When operations were resumed in 1198 one of the monks, Gilbert of Eversolt, was appointed master of the works, or as we should now say, clerk of the works. Money was poured out but little headway was made. Abbot John seemed doomed to frustration and disappointment. The Interdict imposed on this country by Pope Innocent III in John's reign which virtually closed the churches throughout the land from 1208 to 1213, made matters worse. When the abbot refused to celebrate mass in the abbey at the King's command, the monastery was seized by the tyrannical John and the convent fined sums amounting to 1,100 marks, equal to more than £20,000 to-day. The distracted abbot saw but a fraction of the new west front he had planned, for at his death in 1214 only the north porch was finished and the masons were busy on the central porch.

The task of completing the work so grossly mismanaged by Abbot John de Cella fell to his successor, William of Trumpington, 1214–35, though some time elapsed before definite progress was made. When the new west front was in an advanced stage, the old Norman façade was taken down and the masons started on the nave extension. Working from west to east, they put up four bays on the north side of the nave and five on the south side. The westernmost Norman pier of the south arcade was replaced by a new pier and the next to the east was partly remodelled. The existence of vaulting shafts indicates that a high vault of stone was intended but evidently everyone concerned was so anxious to bring the long-drawn-out project to an end that the new bays were roofed with timber. Moreover the idea of erecting western towers was abandoned. Beneath the turf outside the building lie the foundations of the towers, 40 feet square, and at the end of the south aisle is to be seen the lofty arch which would have opened into the south-west tower.

The western extension of the abbey imparted a total internal length of 275 ft. 6 in. to the nave, the longest in any mediaeval church in England.

ARCHITECTURAL CHARACTER OF THE WESTERN EXTENSION

The thirteenth-century west front was subjected to drastic changes in the fifteenth century and what was left was almost entirely obliterated by Lord Grimthorpe. The sole remnants of the original façade are the inner parts of the three porches, which in their complete state must have been a choice example of Early English Gothic. Gilbert Scott, who saw them before the Grimthorpian destruction, doubted whether there was in England 'a work so perfect in art as the half-ruined portals of S. Albans'. The porches have quadripartite vaults and wall-arcading carried by shafts of Purbeck marble. The central portal is double, being divided by a cluster of marble shafts.

Abbot Trumpington's bays of the nave differ in proportions from the Norman bays to the east, the main arches being carried up to a greater height at the expense of the triforium. By the time the new bays were being built Purbeck marble was the architectural fashion, and piers with detached marble shafts were the order of the day; but the Early English piers at S. Albans were built wholly of stone in order that they should harmonize more or less with the plastered piers of the eleventh century. The responds on the western wall of the nave were, however, intended to have five marble shafts, for the annulet rings and bases are still in situ.

On the north side of the nave the junction of the Early English and Norman work is marked by a 'half-and-half' pier, the fourth from the west. The main mass of the pier is Norman, but the upper courses and the capital are the work of Trumpington's masons. From this pier a round arch carrying a wall spans the north aisle to support the aisle roof.

The Early English triforium consists of two main arches in each bay with two sub-arches springing from clustered shafts and profusely enriched with dog-tooth ornament; and the spandrels are pierced with simple forms of plate tracery. In each bay of the clerestory are two Lancet windows but there is an absence of dog-tooth ornament.

As the building of the new bays progressed, the architectural design was somewhat modified. On both sides of the nave the vaulting shafts stop short at the triforium level and were omitted altogether in the eastern bay of the south arcade, the last to be built.

The extension of the nave involved the reconstruction of the extra-mural chapel of S. Andrew at the north-west (see PLAN). When completed it was about 142 feet in length and ranged with the six western

bays of the nave, an arcade of four arches dividing it from the north aisle. The chapel was, however, rebuilt at the cost of the parishioners in 1450–8.

Early in the thirteenth century a school of painters and craftsmen in wood and metal attached itself to the abbey, led by 'the incomparable painter and sculptor', Walter de Colchester, who subsequently entered the monastery and was made sacrist (p. 59). The services and skill of Colchester and his assistants were put to good purpose by Abbot Trumpington, in the embellishment of the abbey church. The sacrist Walter erected a rood-loft in the nave and carved a great Rood with attendant figures of Mary and S. John 'at the cost of the sacristy, yet by his own efforts and industry'. He also made a shrine for the relics of S. Amphibalus which was placed in front of the rood-screen 'handsomely wrought and painted by him'. Of the same period are the reredos paintings on the Norman piers in the nave, which may be attributed to the Colchester family or their fellow-artists. There are two paintings one above the other on the western faces of the piers, the upper depicting the Crucifixion with the Virgin Mary and S. John on either side, and the lower an episode in the life of the Virgin Mary. In the fourteenth century figures of saints were painted on the fronts of the piers (APPENDIX A).

THE REMODELLING OF THE CHOIR

Sooner or later it was inevitable that the choir-arm of the abbey church should undergo an entire remodelling. Long before the middle of the thirteenth century the Norman apsed choir was out of date and inconvenient for the monks' processions, and for the crowds of pilgrims who surged into the church to visit the shrine of S. Alban in the apse behind the High Altar. The pilgrims were difficult to control in the confined space of the sanctuary; a special chapel was needed. Further, the cult of Virgin adoration fostered by Pope, bishop and abbot, made a Lady Chapel a necessity in a great Benedictine church. At Canterbury and Winchester new and commodious eastern arms had been erected, perfectly planned for processional and pilgrimage purposes.

In 1257, owing to the unsafe condition of the Norman apses the long-overdue remodelling of the choir of S. Albans was resolved upon, the lay-out being on

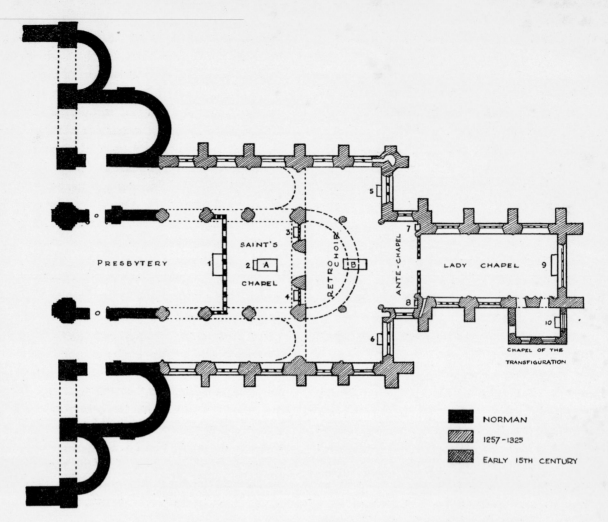

FIG. II. PLAN OF THE REMODELLED EASTERN ARM, 1257–1325

A, *Shrine of S. Alban;* B, *Shrine of S. Amphibalus;* O, *Ostia Presbyterii. Altars:* 1, *High Altar;* 2, *Shrine altar;* 3, *S. Hugh;* 4, *Of the Salutation;* 5, *S. Michael and S. Katherine;* 6, *Our Lady of the Four Tapers;* 7, *S. Edmund;* 8, *S. Peter;* 9, *Our Lady;* 10, *S. Saviour*

the lines of that at Winchester, which had been in use for more than half a century. The plan embraced a spacious sanctuary, a Saint's chapel for S. Alban's shrine behind the High Altar, with aisles leading to a square retrochoir which served as an ambulatory and as a vestibule to the Lady Chapel at the extreme east.

This laudable if not ambitious undertaking, begun by Abbot John de Hertford, 1235–63, occupied more than sixty years, the building operations being held up from time to time for lack of funds. The Lady Chapel, the last part to be erected, was not finished until *c.* 1325 during the rule of Abbot Hugh of Eversden.

The new presbytery together with the Saint's chapel, is of the same length as was the Norman choir; there was no need to extend it eastwards as the ritual choir for the seating of the monks was in the nave and cross-

ing. To safeguard the stability of the central tower the solid walls of the Norman choir* were left standing and were faced with arcading that ranges with the arches to the east.

The High Altar was placed in the fourth bay of the presbytery, and the bay and a half beyond was the chapel of S. Alban, squared at the east by an arcade of three arches opening into the retrochoir. Piers with detached shafts of Purbeck marble might be expected in the remodelled presbytery, but possibly from considerations of cost the stout clustered piers were built wholly of stone. In each bay of the triforium is a range of six blind panels with trefoiled heads and the clerestory has three-light windows of Decorated Gothic that were renewed in the nineteenth century.

* The small doorways (ostia presbyterii) in these walls were remade by Gilbert Scott.

20 · THE JUNCTION OF THE GOTHIC AND NORMAN WORK ON THE NORTH SIDE OF THE NAVE ·
The thirteenth-century masons remodelled only the upper part of the Norman pier and threw
the new arch well above the Norman arches to the right.

19 · NORMAN PIER WITH PAINTING ON THE NORTH SIDE OF THE NAVE · Altars were set up
against the nave piers and in the thirteenth century the surfaces above the altars were adorned
with paintings. On each pier the upper painting represented the Crucifixion.

27

21 · THE NAVE LOOKING EAST FROM TRIFORIUM LEVEL · Beyond the thirteenth-century bays on the left are the Norman bays built by Abbot Paul's masons. Above the rood-screen is seen an arch of the tower and far distant the Wallingford screen.

22 & 23 · NORMAN CAPITALS IN THE SOUTH TRANSEPT · It is evident from these sculptured capitals that the Norman arcading on the south wall, transplanted from the slype, is much later than the transepts themselves.

24 · THE CATHEDRAL FROM THE SOUTH-WEST · The enormous length of the nave, the longest in any English church, is here apparent. Beneath the turf flanking the west front are the foundations of towers never erected.

25 · TOMB WITH ALTAR SLAB IN THE SOUTH AISLE OF THE PRESBYTERY · The slab of Frosterley marble incised with five consecration crosses was probably the mensa of an altar in the chapel of S. Cuthbert now destroyed. (*Below*)

26 · NORMAN DOORWAY IN THE SOUTH TRANSEPT · The portal now in the end wall was transplanted from the slype by Lord Grimthorpe and much new ornament was added 'to bewilder antiquaries'. (*Right*)

28 · SOUTH AISLE OF THE NAVE LOOKING EAST · The piers and arches are part of the early thirteenth-century nave-extension but the vaulting is modern.

27 · NORMAN PLASTERED PIERS FROM THE NORTH AISLE · The crude and somewhat stark piers in the nave were the best the Norman masons could make of Roman bricks and plaster.

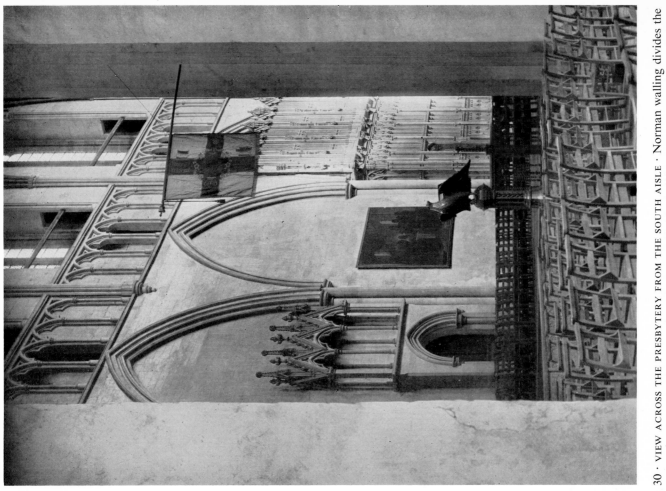

30 · VIEW ACROSS THE PRESBYTERY FROM THE SOUTH AISLE · Norman walling divides the presbytery from the aisles, but the arches were added in the thirteenth century. The small door-way (*ostium presbyterii*) was renewed by Gilbert Scott and the triforium by Lord Grimthorpe.

29 · EARLY ENGLISH TRIFORIUM OF THE NAVE · The slender shafts, bell capitals and mould-ings enriched with dog-tooth ornament are typical of early thirteenth-century architecture.

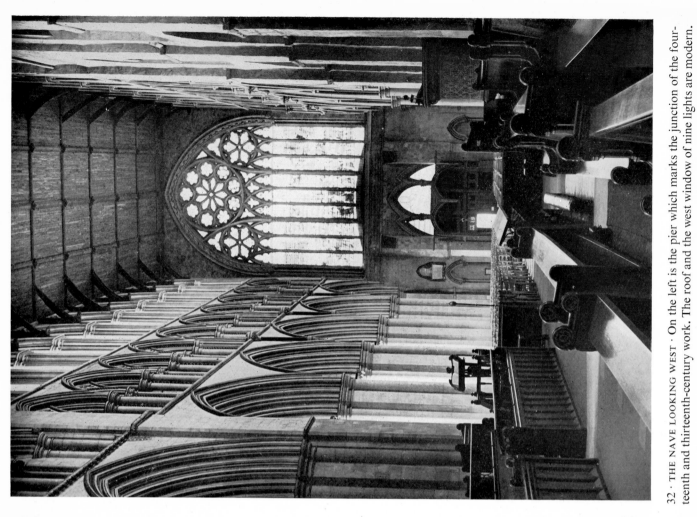

32 · THE NAVE LOOKING WEST · On the left is the pier which marks the junction of the fourteenth and thirteenth-century work. The roof and the west window of nine lights are modern.

31 · THIRTEENTH-CENTURY BAYS OF THE NAVE FROM THE SOUTH AISLE · In their shafted piers, arch-mouldings and elegant triforium, the Early English bays afford a striking contrast with the Norman work to the east.

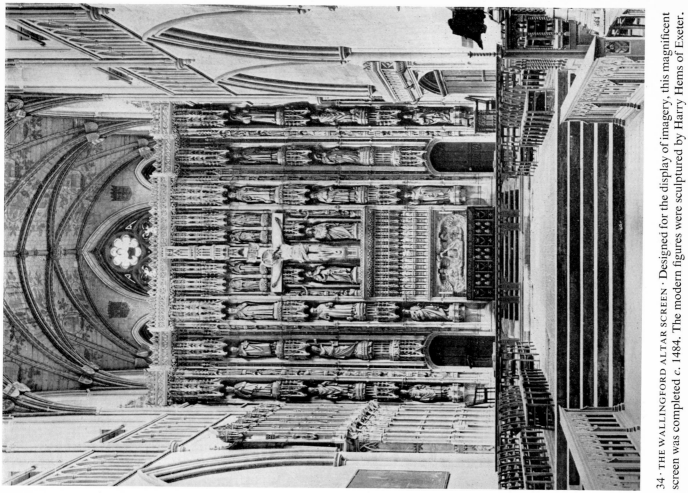

34 · THE WALLINGFORD ALTAR SCREEN · Designed for the display of imagery, this magnificent screen was completed c. 1484. The modern figures were sculptured by Harry Hems of Exeter.

33 · ROOF OF THE PRESBYTERY · The wooden vault dates from the late thirteenth century, but the painted roundels and other decoration are of the fifteenth century.

35 · THE SAINT'S CHAPEL FROM THE SOUTH · Countless pilgrims visited the chapel to gaze upon the shrine of S. Alban, the pedestal of which stands in the centre. Beyond is the watching-house.

34

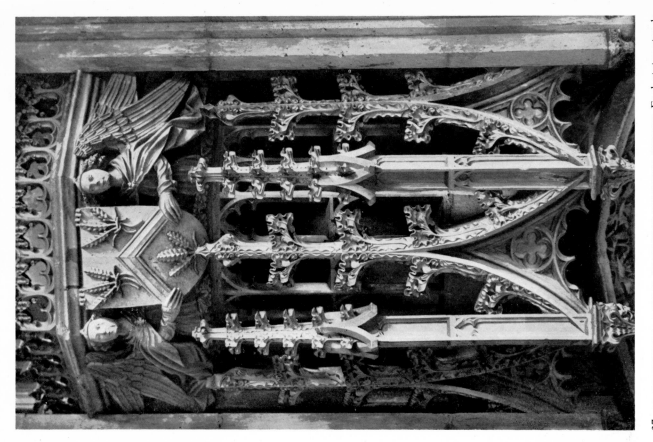

37 · ARCHITECTURAL DETAIL OF THE WALLINGFORD SCREEN · Each statue stands in a niche with an elaborate canopy above and angels supporting heraldic arms.

36 · TOWER ARCH AT THE WEST END OF THE SOUTH AISLE · Early in the thirteenth century this lofty and richly moulded archway was erected, to open into a south-western tower that was abandoned.

38 · DETAIL OF THE WALLINGFORD SCREEN · The main figures are disposed in three tiers of niches, those seen here being S. Helen and S. Benedict. (*Left*)

39 · SCULPTURE ON THE SHRINE · In the gable at the west end is a representation of the martyrdom of S. Alban with censing angels above. (*Right*)

40 · THE PEDESTAL OF S. ALBAN'S SHRINE · The pedestal which was made early in the fourteenth century, was broken up at the Reformation but reconstructed in 1872. On the top was placed the feretrum containing the saint's remains.

41 · SOUTH AISLE OF THE PRESBYTERY FROM THE EAST · The two western bays of the aisle have groined vaults; the Decorated arcading on the wall to the left is modern.

42 · THE WATCHING-HOUSE FROM THE NORTH · On both sides the upper floor projects, and on the aisle side is backed with solid panels to protect the monk-watchers from draughts.

43 · THE WALLINGFORD CHANTRY CHAPEL · The single-arched chapel south of the High Altar is usually attributed to Abbot Wheat-hampstead, but Sir Charles Peers has shown that it was founded by Abbot Wallingford.

45 · CLOISTER DOORWAY IN THE SOUTH AISLE · Dating from the second half of the fourteenth century, the portal is a good example of Decorated Gothic. In the arch spandrels are heraldic shields of Richard II and the abbey.

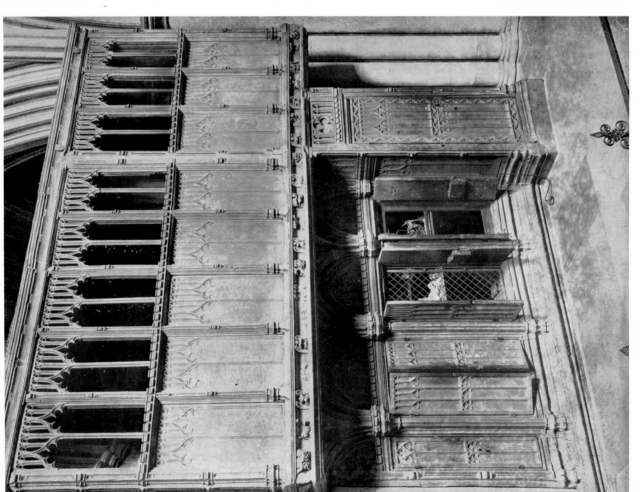

44 · THE WATCHING-HOUSE IN THE SAINT'S CHAPEL · Early in the fifteenth century the two-storied house of timber was built for the monk-guards who watched the Saint's chapel by day and night. The upper floor was the watching-chamber, beneath which are cupboards for storing relics, plate and vestments.

47 · THE SHRINE OF S. AMPHIBALUS · Originally constructed c. 1350, the pedestal was destroyed at the Reformation but the fragments were pieced together when the retrochoir was restored by Gilbert Scott.

46 · THE NORTH AISLE OF THE PRESBYTERY LOOKING EAST · To the left and near the screen is the reconstructed pedestal of the shrine of S. Amphibalus and opposite is the watching-house. On the right is the Ramryge chapel.

48 · THE RETROCHOIR LOOKING WEST · The retrochoir is planned with a central area and aisles. Here formerly stood the shrine of S. Amphibalus. Through the three arches is obtained a glimpse of the saint's chapel.

49 · ALTAR OF OUR LADY OF THE FOUR TAPERS · The ancient altar in the south aisle of the retrochoir was restored in 1931 by the Mothers' Union of the diocese of S. Albans.

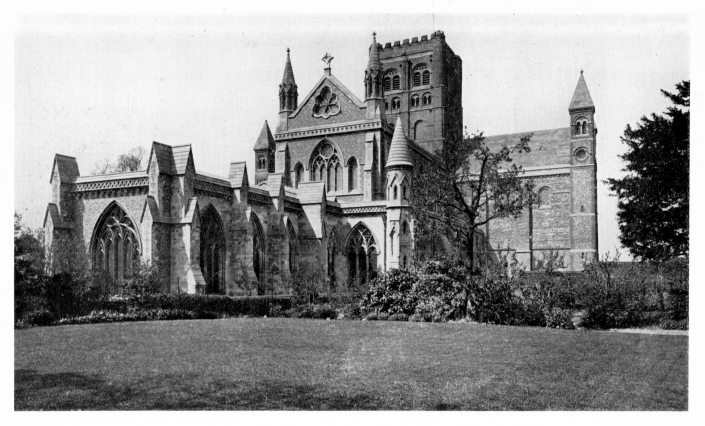

50 · THE CATHEDRAL FROM THE NORTH-EAST · The big remodelling of the eastern arm begun in 1257 is seen at a glance—the Lady Chapel, retrochoir, aisles and presbytery. It was drastically restored in the nineteenth century.

51 · THE LADY CHAPEL FROM THE WEST · Despite mutilations and restorations, the Lady Chapel, which is 57 feet long and was completed *c.* 1325, remains one of the most beautiful parts of the cathedral. The vault and wall-arcading were Lord Grimthorpe's.

52 · SEDILIA AND TABERNACLING IN THE LADY CHAPEL · Though much restored, the decorated sedilia and tabernacling in the south-east corner of the chapel are features of no little beauty and interest. (*Left*)

53 · WALL-ARCADING IN THE LADY CHAPEL · The naturalistic capitals and stops of the new arcading were carved by John Baker during the restoration. (*Right*)

54 · THE FOURTEENTH-CENTURY BAYS OF THE NAVE · The collapse of two Norman bays on the south side of the nave in 1323 necessitated the rebuilding of five bays, the general design of which resembles that of the Early English bays to the west,

It must have been the intention of the masons to erect a high vault of stone, the springers of which are still in position in the clerestory wall, and there is external evidence that flying buttresses were contemplated. But the building was roofed with a quadripartite ceiling of wood to which colour decoration was applied in the fifteenth century.

THE SHRINE OF S. ALBAN

As soon as the Saint's chapel was ready, Abbot John de Maryns, 1302–8, 'moved and adorned the shrine of S. Alban'. The precious feretrum was placed on the lofty pedestal or 'throne', now pieced together and restored to its rightful position in the centre of the Saint's chapel. The pedestal is made of Purbeck marble and is 8 ft. 3 in. in height and about the same in length. In each side are four gabled niches into which sick persons were wont to crouch in hope of a miraculous cure. The backs of the niches are enriched with curvilinear tracery which was treated with colour, mainly vermilion and blue. In the basement are quatrefoil panels, two of them pierced with lozenge-shaped openings into which the crippled thrust their limbs to absorb the healing virtues of S. Alban's bones. The stonework above the niches is carved with foliage, and in the gables are sculptured representations of the life of S. Alban; and the spandrels above are occupied by censing angels and seated kings. At the western end is 'The Martyrdom of S. Alban' and beneath was formerly an altar dedicated to the saint. Amongst the kingly figures on the south side is one of Offa holding a model of a church. The pedestal is surmounted with cresting. The bases remain of fourteen detached marble shafts that stood around the shrine before the Reformation. Covering the feretrum was a wooden canopy suspended from a pulley in the roof by chains, so that it could be raised easily on the occasion of an exposition. On the two festivals of S. Alban and on Ascension Day, the feretrum was taken from its throne and carried in procession round the church by four priests. At the Suppression it was despoiled of its precious metals and jewels and the pedestal broken up, but in 1872 more than two thousand fragments of the pedestal were discovered in the retrochoir and with amazing skill were reassembled by the clerk of the works,

some plain stone being used for the missing pieces; so that to-day the pedestal presents us with the form and design of the original, though its former splendour and magnificence is left to our imagination.

When the eastern arm of the abbey was being remodelled it was a simple matter to remove the lateral apses and extend the aisles into the retrochoir.

Of the actual fabric of the thirteenth-century retrochoir little has survived, for soon after the abbey was suppressed a right-of-way was cut athwart it from north to south and the restoration of 1874 almost amounted to a complete rebuilding. The outer walls, windows, wall-arcadings and timber ceilings are therefore modern.

Roofed at a lower level than the presbytery, the retrochoir is divided into a nave and aisles by arcades of two arches springing from octagonal columns, and at the east is a narrow bay which serves as an ante-chapel to the Lady Chapel. Early in the fourteenth century the retrochoir was ready for its altars. One dedicated to S. Michael was placed at the eastern extremity of the north aisle, and in the corresponding position on the south was the altar of Our Lady of the Tapers. The latter was re-erected in 1931 by the Mothers' Union of the diocese of S. Albans. The Renaissance altar-piece with its coupled Corinthian columns and the four angels bearing tapers has certainly added a use and interest to this part of the retrochoir. Altars were also set up in the ante-chapel, the northern dedicated to S. Edmund, king and martyr and the southern to S. Peter (Fig. II).

THE LADY CHAPEL

The chronicles relate that Abbot Hugh of Eversden, 1308–26, 'brought to a praiseworthy completion the chapel of the Virgin in the eastern part of the church'. On Hugh's accession the walls had only risen to a height of six feet. In its original state the Lady Chapel, which is 57 feet long and 24 feet wide, was a lovely example of Decorated Gothic, lighted with curvilinear windows, whose mullions and jambs are adorned with small figures of saints, kings and queens. Ball-flower ornament occurs in the jambs. The east window of five lights is an unusual combination of Decorated tracery and crocketed gables. The original arcading beneath the windows was so badly mutilated by the grammar school boys of three centuries, that new arcading had to be applied to the walls during restoration. Abbot Hugh roofed the chapel with an imitation vault of timber, that has been replaced by a tierceron vault of stone. When completed the Lady Chapel was enclosed at the west by a timber screen.

Beneath the floor of the Lady Chapel were buried Edmund Beaufort Duke of Somerset, Henry Percy Earl of Northumberland, Thomas Lord Clifford and other Lancastrian nobles who were slain at the first battle of S. Albans in May 1455; and three years afterwards as an earnest of reconciliation, the Duke of York and the Earls of Salisbury and Warwick undertook to found a chantry in the abbey for the souls of the Lancastrians who had fallen in the battle. An endowment of £45 a year was made to support the chantry.

Abbot Hugh of Eversden also fitted up the ritual choir with new stalls, for which Edward II presented the convent with a quantity of timber and 100 marks. The stalls which have long since disappeared were executed by a Master Geoffrey and were lofty structures. As can be seen, the two western piers at the crossing were cut back to a considerable height to take the tabernacling that surmounted the seats.

THE CALAMITY OF 1323

The content that filled the hearts of the abbot and his brethren now that the big reconstruction was at an end, was rudely shattered by a calamity that befell the abbey church in 1323. Immediately after the celebration of a mass at the altar of the Virgin Mary in the nave on S. Paulinus day, 10 October, the fourth and fifth piers of the south nave arcade west of the crossing crashed outwards and the fall of the superstructure wrecked the south aisle and the adjoining cloister-walk. Shortly afterwards the roof of the nave collapsed. Though a great number of people were in the nave at the time, no one was injured, but a timber beam fell on the shrine of S. Amphibalus in front of the rood-screen and broke the marble shafts supporting the canopy. Miraculously the feretrum was unharmed.

Without delay, the work of reparation was put in hand by Abbot Hugh under the direction of Henry Wy, 'magister opertum'. Five bays of the south arcade

of the nave, the fourth to the eighth inclusive, had to be rebuilt as well as the ruined aisle and cloister-walk. Unfortunately the progress of the work was retarded by the death of Abbot Hugh, and his successor, the dilatory Richard of Wallingford, 1326–34, was more engrossed in the study of astronomy and in the making of a wonderful clock than in the restoration of the nave. When Edward III visited the abbey and watched him toying with the mechanism of his clock, the king suggested that he would be better employed in getting the nave finished, whereupon the abbot replied that anyone could repair the church but only he could make the clock.

For twenty years the rebuilding dragged on and was not completed until c. 1345. Abbot Michael de Mentmore, 1335–49, who acquired the quarries of Eglemount for the supply of stone, roofed the new bays of the south aisle with quadripartite vaults.

THE DECORATED BAYS OF THE NAVE

In general design the fourteenth-century bays of the nave are similar to the Early English bays to the west. The proportions of the three stages are the same, but in the detail the advance to Decorated Gothic is at once apparent. The piers are of the same form and size but the arch-mouldings are 'thinner' than the bold rounds and hollows of the thirteenth century. From east to west the hood-moulds terminate in carved heads of Abbot Hugh, Queen Isabella, Edward II and master-mason Geoffrey, and in the arch-spandrels are shields bearing the arms of England, Edward the Confessor, Mercia and France. In the triforium the sub-arches are cusped, the hood-moulds have head-stops and foliage capitals and ball-flower ornaments appear in place of the bell-capitals and dog-tooth of the Early English triforium.

At the junction of the Decorated and Early English bays is a massive pier with a broad pilaster on its northern face that is continued up to the roof. Against this pier Abbot Michael de Mentmore placed the altar of 'Our Lady of the Pillar' and enclosed the area to the west with iron grilles, to make a chapel for the Guild of S. Alban. Altars dedicated to the Virgin Mary, S. Thomas of Canterbury and S. Benedict were erected against others of the new piers, but about twenty years later they were removed to positions against the rood-screen.

THE BLACK DEATH

The convent suffered terribly from the Black Death, which swept over this country in 1349. The pestilence carried off Abbot Michael de Mentmore, the prior, the sub-prior and forty-five of the monks. Hitherto S. Albans, as the premier Benedictine monastery in the land, had been a house of the religious *élite*; Abbot John de Cella had been obliged to limit the number of monks to a hundred, but after the Black Death the convent rarely numbered sixty.

THE SHRINE OF AMPHIBALUS

When the nave fell in 1323 the undamaged feretrum of S. Amphibalus was removed to the north aisle of the presbytery and there remained until 1350, when the sacrist Ralph Whitchurch translated the relics to a new 'throne' in the middle of the retrochoir (Fig. II). It was enclosed within an iron grating 'where had been fixed a decent altar with a painting and other suitable ornaments', and was reconsecrated by the Irish Bishop of Ardfert. Abbot de la Mare, 1349–96, adorned the shrine with images and silver-gilt plates at a cost of £8. 8s. 10d. At the Dissolution the pedestal was broken up and the masonry used for walling up the eastern arches of the Saint's chapel, but when Gilbert Scott restored the retrochoir the fragments were put together to make the full-sized but imperfect replica now in the north aisle of the presbytery. In the sides are two gabled recesses and the initials of the sacrist appear in the diaper-ornament of the base. At the western end of the pedestal a few letters of the Saint's name are carved in the masonry.

THE FOURTEENTH-CENTURY ROOD-SCREEN

It is reasonable to assume that but for the Black Death, Abbot Michael de Mentmore would have erected a new rood-screen in the nave to replace the one damaged by the disaster of 1323. To his successor, Thomas de la Mare, is attributed the present rood-screen of stone which spans the nave, three bays west of the crossing. At the time of his election, de la Mare was prior of Tynemouth and he ruled at S. Albans for forty-seven years, from 1349 to 1396. Other additions of his still remaining are the cloister doorway and the Great Gatehouse of the abbey, but he demolished the Norman apses in the south transept to provide a site for two vestries, long since destroyed.

The rood-screen, dating *c.* 1363–5, is built of clunch and is 43 feet long from north to south and 22 feet high. In all probability it extended across the aisles so as to isolate the monks' part of the church. Against the screen were placed three altars; in the centre stood the altar of Our Lady flanked by a processional doorway on each side, and the lateral altars were dedicated to S. Thomas of Canterbury and S. Benedict. The front of the screen is adorned with canopied niches above the altars and panelling over the doorways and though divested of the all-important statuary and colour it is notwithstanding one of the finest extant.

The cloister portal at the east end of the south aisle is an ornate example of Decorated Gothic, with rich carvings in the arch-mouldings and in the recesses flanking the door. In the spandrels appear heraldic shields of Richard II and the abbey, and the cornice and cresting unify the whole design.

THE WATCHING-HOUSE IN THE SAINT'S CHAPEL

From time to time ornaments of great value were lavished upon the shrine of S. Alban. Thus, Abbot de la Mare embellished the feretrum with a silver-gilt turret and a silver eagle with outspread wings, and one of the monks, Richard Savage, presented two silver-gilt suns whose rays were tipped with precious stones. The bejewelled shrine had to be protected from common thieves; and the bones of the saint and other relics were liable to be stolen by covetous monks of other houses. Day and night the keeper of the shrine, assisted by monk-guards, kept a close watch over the treasures in the Saint's chapel. Early in the fifteenth century a timber watching-house was erected on the north side of the chapel for the comfort of the guards during the long watches of the night. It is a two-storied structure, 17 feet high and is built of oak. At the east end is a stairway up to the watching-loft, whence a commanding view is obtained of the whole of the Saint's chapel. The front of the loft is panelled up to half its height and above are two-light Perpendicular windows, unglazed. The lower story consists of cupboards where were stored relics, palls, vestments and other valuables. The woodwork is noteworthy for its carved detail. In the deep moulding between the two stories are carvings of the martyrdom of S. Alban, Time the Reaper, the seasons and the hart of Richard II, and on the aisle side appear the occupations of the months. It is recorded that Robert of Malton made a gift of 200 marks towards the building of this unique watching-house which was being used by the monk-guards in 1420.

That same year John of Wheathampstead became abbot of S. Albans. He resigned in 1440 but twelve years afterwards he was re-elected and retained the abbacy until his death in 1465. During the first period of his rule, the abbot built the little chapel of the Transfiguration at the south-eastern angle of the Lady Chapel. It was dedicated in 1430 but was entirely rebuilt in the nineteenth century. Several minor alterations were made in the church by Abbot Wheathampstead. To improve the lighting of the nave he tore down part of the Early English west front and inserted a large Perpendicular window of nine lights, the tracery of which had been brought from the north of England; and at the same time the roofs of the aisles were lowered so that light would enter the nave by the triforium openings.

A more urgent task was the reconditioning of the roofs of the transepts and nave, the old timbers of which were in a state of decay. Further, the flat ceiling of the ritual choir and the timber vaulting of the presbytery were decorated with paintings. Those on the sixty-six square panels of the choir-ceiling consist of the sacred monogram I H S alternating with heraldic shields of Edward III and his kinsfolk, and in the centre the Coronation of the Virgin. On the presbytery vault are roundels of the lamb of S. John Baptist and the eagle of S. John Evangelist, which were adopted by the abbot as his personal badges.

In Wheathampstead's time the Norman apses in the north transept were taken down, no doubt because they were ruinous. The abbot founded a chantry chapel 'outside the south aisle of the presbytery in the monks' cemetery'. The doorway of the chapel is to be seen in the wall opposite the Saint's chapel and the foundations were unearthed in 1846.

In the early years of the fifteenth century, the abbey came under the patronage of Humphrey, Duke of Gloucester, son of Henry IV and Protector of the Realm during the minority of his nephew, Henry VI. The Duke was a close friend of Abbot Wheathampstead and spent much time at S. Albans. The story is told by Sir Thomas More of the Duke's detection of an impostor who claimed to have been born blind and to have received his sight at S. Alban's shrine, an incident dramatized by Shakespeare in *Henry VI*, *Part II*. In 1441 Duke Humphrey made over the alien priory of Pembroke to the abbot and convent of S. Albans for the endowment of a chantry in the abbey church. Provision was made for the celebration of a daily mass on behalf of the Duke, for the distribution of alms and for the payment of £60 a year to the monks' kitchen. The 'Good Duke Humphrey' was murdered in 1447 by William de la Pole, Duke of Suffolk, with the connivance of Queen Margaret and Cardinal Beaufort. A chapel was built for his chantry on the south side of the Saint's chapel and his body was buried within a few feet of the shrine. In such esteem was he held that 'the abbot and convent . . . payed, for the makynge of the tomb and place of sepulture of the saide Duke within the said monasterie, the summe of £433 6*s*. 8*d*.'. His chantry chapel, built in two stories, is one of the most splendid in the country, an elaborate specimen of Perpendicular Gothic. The lower stage with open sides was designed to house the tomb of the Duke and is spanned by three pendant arches. Within is a fan vault and in the cornice are four shields displaying the arms of Humphrey, supported by chained antelopes. Niches alternate with traceried panels on the fronts of the upper floor, the niches on the south side being tenanted by seventeen small figures of kings. The chapel is fenced on the aisle side with a grille of Sussex ironwork dating from the end of the thirteenth century. Under the pavement of the Saint's chapel and reached by a flight of steps is a vault where the remains of the Duke were discovered in 1703 enclosed in a leaden coffin and on the wall of the vault was a painting of the Crucifixion.

The great Perpendicular window in the west front revealed the glory of the nave so effectually that similar windows were inserted in the end walls of the transepts by Abbot William of Wallingford, 1476–84. That in the south transept was 24 feet wide. Both windows were taken out about sixty years ago, but a more important work of Abbot Wallingford's, viz., the magnificent stone screen behind the High Altar, has fortunately been spared.

THE WALLINGFORD SCREEN

No more appropriate background was ever devised for the supreme act of Christian worship than the Wallingford screen which rises some 40 feet to the level of the clerestory. It was designed for the display of painted imagery and when completed, *c.* 1484, presented a glorious array of saints and kings, resplendent in colour and gold and surmounted by a mass of sumptuous tabernacling. All the original statues were destroyed by the iconoclasts of the sixteenth century; those now occupying the niches were made by Harry Hems of Exeter during Grimthorpe's restoration, and the relief-sculpture of the Resurrection that forms the reredos of the High Altar was the work of Sir Alfred Gilbert, R.A. The centre-piece is a large crucifix with figures of the Virgin Mary and S. John on either side and below is a row of small niches containing alabaster figures of Our Lord and the apostles.

The main statuary is arranged in three tiers of canopied niches and a number of small figures of the lesser saints are tucked away in the slender buttresses dividing the screen into vertical compartments. From left to right the larger statues in the top tier represent King Edmund, King Offa II, S. Edward Confessor, S. Hugh of Lincoln, Pope Adrian IV and the Venerable Beda; in the middle row, S. Cuthbert of Durham, S. Helen, S. Benedict, S. Patrick, S. Etheldreda of Ely, and S. Germain; and in the bottom tier are S. Augustine, S. Alban, S. Amphibalus and S. Erkenwald.

On each side of the altar is a door that opens into the Saint's chapel and was used exclusively by the monks. The Wallingford screen is built of clunch and cost 1,100 marks, a sum equivalent to more than £20,000 to-day.*

On the south side of the sanctuary, adjoining the

* Bishop Fox's screen at Winchester is obviously a copy of this at S. Albans and may have been made in the same 'shop'.

High Altar is a low chantry chapel usually attributed to Abbot Wheathampstead, though Sir Charles Peers has shown from documentary evidence that it was founded by Abbot Wallingford. 'For the building of his chapel and tomb on the south near the High Altar, with railings and marble slab with a figure set on it . . . he [Abbot Wallingford] expended £100.' (V.C.H., Herts) There is no tomb in the chapel to confirm this, but as Abbot Wheathampstead had already built a chantry chapel (dedicated in 1430) outside the south choir aisle, it is unlikely that he founded another. Architecturally, the Wallingford chapel is undistinguished, its main features being the canopy carried by a deep four-centred arch with panelled soffit and the iron grilles on either side. In the cornice is carved the motto 'Valles habundabunt' with three wheat-ears, and in the quatrefoiled panels above are the rose-en-soleil, the arms of S. George, and a mitre with a wheat-ear. The rose-en-soleil was the badge of Edward IV and it can therefore be assumed that the chapel was built between 1471 and 1483. In the chapel is preserved a Flemish brass which covered the grave of Abbot de la Mare, *d.* 1396, in front of the High Altar. It was engraved *c.* 1367 and is one of the largest and most splendid in England. The Abbot is portrayed wearing mitre and vestments and holding the pastoral staff.

THE RAMRYGE CHAPEL

On the north side of the sanctuary is the stately chantry chapel of Abbot Thomas Ramryge, 1492–1521, the last addition to the abbey church before the Suppression. Two stories in height, the chapel completely fills the arch in which it stands. The lower stage is enclosed by stone screens of three-light windows above a panelled base and the cornice is enriched with carvings of the abbot's rebus, a ram wearing a collar which bears the letters 'RYGE'. The rams support the arms of S. Albans, Henry VIII and the cells of the abbey. The front of the upper story has rectilinear panelling alternating with canopied niches and resembles that of Duke Humphrey's chapel. In the spandrels of the doorway at the south-west are sculptures representing the scourging and martyrdom of S. Alban. Within the lower stage, the chapel proper, is a charming fan-vault and a stone slab is preserved, incised with a figure of Abbot Ramryge and a Latin inscription on the verge. There is an abundance of delicately carved detail in the stonework, including foliage, flowers and the emblems of the Passion.

TOMBS AND MEMORIALS

Other than the foregoing chantry chapels there are few mediaeval monuments or memorials in the cathedral. Here and there in the pavement of the presbytery are grave-slabs of abbots and benefactors but the brasses have nearly all been ripped off. There are said to have been two hundred such memorials, of which only a few have survived. In front of the altar-rail, the brasses of Robert Beauner, a monk, d. 1460 and of Sir Anthony Grey, c. 1480, remain undisturbed and before the High Altar are stones marking the burial places of Abbots Hugh of Eversden, Richard of Wallingford, Michael de Mentmore and Thomas de la Mare.

To the west of the cloister doorway in the south aisle is an arched recess of the thirteenth century which is reputed to be the burial place of two hermits, Roger and Sigar, noted for their sanctity of life in the twelfth century. Roger dwelt in a cell at Markyate and Sigar lived in a wood at Northaw, and the legends of their conflicts with the evil one made their sepulchre a place of pilgrimage in the Middle Ages. In the north transept are two modern memorials, an altar-tomb to Bishop Blomfield of Colchester, d. 1884, and a recumbent effigy of Bishop Claughton, 1877–92, the first to occupy the newly created see of S. Albans.

THE ABBEY CHURCH SINCE THE REFORMATION

The abbey of S. Albans with all its possessions was surrendered to the rapacious Henry VIII in December 1539 (p. 60). Through the centuries it had amassed a great quantity of plate, chalices, sacred vessels, rings and vestments, and above all, jewels and ornaments of gold and silver that bedecked the shrines of S. Alban and S. Amphibalus. Within a fortnight of the surrender all the valuables were carted away to London and deposited in the royal jewel house. The plunder yielded 122½ oz. of gold, 2,990 oz. of silver-gilt plate and more than 1,100 oz. of silver.

Intent on purging the abbey church of all that savoured of superstition and idolatry, the zealous reformer now indulged in an orgy of destruction. The pedestals of the shrines were broken up, the relics scattered and lost, altars thrown down, screens destroyed and paintings whitewashed. The imagery which graced the rood-screen and the altar-screen was torn from the niches and the painted glass of the windows shattered.

The church remained Crown property until 1553, when Edward VI conferred a charter on the town and the burgesses purchased it for the nominal sum of £400, and used it henceforward as their parish church. The chapel of S. Andrew being redundant was taken down and as the nave and choir of the monastic church sufficed for parochial needs, the Lady Chapel and part of the retrochoir were converted into a grammar school. A passage was cut through the retrochoir and was walled up on each side to make a right-of-way.

For the next three centuries the treatment of the abbey church was deplorable. To maintain so large a building in a state of good repair was indeed a heavy burden for the townspeople and royal grants were frequently being made and money collected to pay for essential repairs of the fabric. By the middle of the nineteenth century general decay pervaded the whole church and the long disused nave was in a dilapidated condition.

In 1856 Gilbert Scott was entrusted with the task, one which brooked no delay, of undertaking a thorough restoration. His prime concern was to strengthen the foundations, and the need of reinforcing the fabric was emphasized while that was being done. Grave cause for alarm manifested itself in July 1870 when the central tower showed signs of cracking up and collapsing. It was immediately shored up with timber and walling, and examination revealed that the rubble core of the two eastern piers at the crossing had decrepitated under the enormous weight of the tower, and in the south-eastern pier was a huge cavity filled with decaying timber. For some months the work of stabilizing the piers caused great anxiety; the rubble and the rotten timbers were replaced by brickwork and cement and the tower was clamped by iron rods and made secure for a long time to come.

In 1870 the retrochoir and Lady Chapel were re-covered to the church, the right-of-way was closed, the grammar school transferred to the Great Gate-house and the restoration of the east end put in hand. It proved to be a lengthy undertaking. When the work had been in progress seven years the see of S. Albans was created and thus after centuries of neglect the ancient abbey church came into its own and was made the cathedral of the new diocese, though it still retains its status as a parish church. In June 1877 Bishop Claughton of Rochester was enthroned as Bishop of S. Albans. But the restoration of the church was still far from complete. The western bays of the south aisle were vaulted by Gilbert Scott, the window tracery of the Lady Chapel was refaced externally and the tabernacling applied to the walling above the ostia presbyterii. There was work to be done in the nave where the clerestory wall at the south-west was heel-ing over. Gilbert Scott died in 1878 and the cathedral was rashly committed to the tender mercies of Lord Grimthorpe who seems to have been given *carte blanche* in the treatment of the fabric. Few people who wander through the cathedral to-day are aware of the mutilations and architectural shams the noble lord was guilty of, particularly in the transepts and the west front. The latter, then in a ruinous condition, was completely transformed; the whole of the upper part including Wheathampstead's great window was pulled down and a new façade of make-believe Gothic substituted. Only the inner portions of the three Early English porches were spared. The Grimthorp-ian innovations in the nave and aisles, perhaps less apparent, were equally destructive. The exterior wall of the south aisle was largely refaced with flint and brick, new Decorated windows inserted, the three eastern bays were vaulted and buttresses built that cut into the cloister wall-arcading in a most unsightly manner. Grimthorpe also framed the cloister door in a gabled porch; he rebuilt the aisle-wall at the north-west of the nave and extended the rood-screen across the north aisle. The fourteenth-century piers of the nave were found to be unsound due to their defective core and after rebuilding them Grimthorpe shame-lessly declared: 'It took no small trouble and scolding to get the new stones worked as roughly as the old ones, so as to make the work homogeneous and *be-wilder antiquaries*.' (*S. Albans Cathedral and its Restoration.*)

The transepts fared as badly. The Norman octag-onal turrets at the angles were replaced by square turrets, the end wall of the south transept was re-constructed and beneath his five new Lancet windows Grimthorpe placed a Norman doorway and wall-arcading he transplanted from the slype outside. Of the ornament round the doorway he glibly remarked that he had taken 'an unusual amount of trouble to get the carving done so well that people guess wrongly which are old and which are new stones, *which makes antiquaries very angry though it is what everybody wants and seldom gets*'. Of such stuff were the Gothic restorers of the nineteenth century!

The huge circular window in the north transept is Grimthorpe at his worst and the less said about it the better. In the presbytery, the triforium and the cleres-tory windows are reproductions of the originals but the windows in the east wall are Grimthorpe's own creations. The Lady Chapel was restored with a less heavy hand and is now one of the loveliest portions of the cathedral. Of great beauty are the naturalistic capitals of the new wall-arcading carved by John Baker. Flowers and fruit, the primrose and pansy, the gooseberry and pear are rendered in stone with an amazing fidelity to nature.

The mutilations and disfigurements that the cathe-dral suffered in the nineteenth century may have im-paired its worth as a monument of mediaeval archi-tecture, but as a monument of the Christian faith hallowed by nearly nine centuries of prayer and thanksgiving S. Albans compares with any church in the land.

THE MEDIAEVAL MONASTERY
AND THE CONVENTUAL BUILDINGS

Personnel of the abbey in Saxon days · Importance of the house in the twelfth century · A seat of learning and a school of the arts and crafts · Matthew Paris the historian · The Colchester family of artists at S. Albans · Printing · The monks and the townspeople · The Peasants' Revolt · The Wars of the Roses · Last days of the monastery · Abbot Robert Catton, 1530–8 · The surrender in December 1539 · The conventual buildings

LIKE MANY OTHER MONASTERIES of Saxon times, the abbey founded by Offa II was a dual establishment, for nuns as well as monks. It was 'always distinctly an aristocratic house. All the Saxon abbots were drawn from the nobility and many of them were kinsmen of reigning monarchs.' (V.C.H., *Herts.*, IV)

The abbey was reformed by Paul the Norman, and in the twelfth century its fame and repute were such, that under the rule of Robert of Gorham, 1151–66, some of the monks were advanced to abbacies, Germanus to Selby, Godfrey to Crowland and Lawrence to Westminster. In accordance with S. Benedict's injunction that the religious of his Order should cultivate learning, Abbot Geoffrey of Gorham 1119–46 would admit none to the community who were unlettered. Amongst those refused admission was a young man, Nicholas Brakspear of Abbots Langley, whose father, already a monk of S. Albans, desired him to enter the convent. The son was rejected on account of his lack of learning. 'Wait, my son,' said the abbot, 'but go on with your schooling until you become more fit.' Nicholas made good and in 1154 occupied the Papal chair under the name of Adrian IV. He bore no ill-will to the house that had rejected him but raised it to the dignity of a mitred abbey and granted the convent exemption from the jurisdiction of the Bishop of Lincoln, in whose diocese S. Albans was then situated.

During Abbot Geoffrey's rule, S. Albans ceased to be a dual monastery. A Benedictine house was founded for the displaced nuns at Sopwell, less than a mile distant, and all through the Middle Ages the nunnery of S. Mary was closely associated with the parent body.

The abbey became pre-eminent as a seat of learning and a school of arts and crafts in the thirteenth century. In the scriptorium was established the foremost school of mediaeval historians in England; the chief sources of the early history of S. Albans are the chronicles of Roger Wendover, the monk-historiographer, d. 1236, and of his more famous successor, Matthew Paris. The latter continued the *Chronica Majora* of Wendover and compiled *Historia Anglorum* and the *Vitae XXIII abbatum S. Albani* as well as other works. In 1247 Matthew Paris was chosen to instruct the monks of S. Benet Holm in Norway in the Benedictine code, and when Henry III visited S. Albans in 1257 on the Feast of S. Edward of Westminster, Paris conversed and sat at meat with his royal visitor, who enjoined him to write 'a special and full account of the proceedings in a fair writing, indelibly in a book so that the memory of them be not lost by any length of time'.

In the next century, Thomas de Walsingham, the precentor, compiled the *Gesta Abbatum* in which he incorporated much of the writings of Matthew Paris. To foster literary and artistic pursuits in the cloister Abbot de la Mare, in 1351, ordained that the monks

55 · TRIFORIUM OF THE NAVE · The flat pilaster divides the Decorated work from that of the Early English period. The cusped arches, foliage capitals and head-stop on the left show an advance on the simpler design with dog-tooth ornament on the right.

56 · THE STOUP IN THE WESTERN WALL · The holy water stoup of the Decorated period that is now built in the western wall of the nave was originally in the northern porch of the west front.

57 · A DECORATED CAPITAL IN THE TRIFORIUM OF THE NAVE · How closely the carver of the fourteenth century imitated natural foliage is evidenced from the leafage of the triforium capital.

58 · THE ROOD-SCREEN IN THE NAVE · The rood-screen which was erected c. 1363 and is 22 feet high, originally had altars flanking the doorways in addition to the central altar shown here.

60 · DETAIL OF THE ROOD-SCREEN · To the right of the door stood the altar of S. Thomas of Canterbury. The doorway and walling above are modern.

59 · ABBOT RAMRYGE'S CHANTRY CHAPEL · The chapel which was built c. 1510 is an exquisite example of Perpendicular Gothic. Within, masses were recited for the abbot's soul.

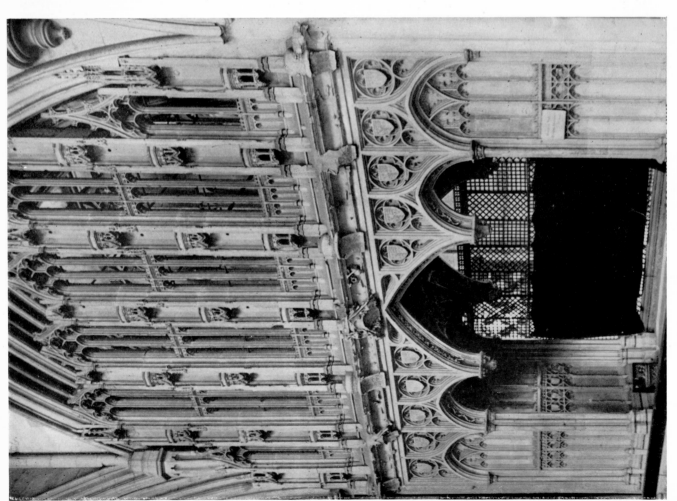

62 · THE FAN-VAULT OF DUKE HUMPHREY'S CHAPEL · The fan-vault with pendants in the lower stage of the chapel is a marvel of mediaeval stone-cutting.

61 · DUKE HUMPHREY'S CHAPEL · The two-storied chapel of Humphrey, Duke of Gloucester, d. 1447, stands on the south side of the Saint's chapel. In the cornice are shields displaying the arms of the Duke.

64 · DUKE HUMPHREY'S CHAPEL FROM THE SOUTH · A thirteenth century grille encloses the-chapel on this side. The doorway opens into the Saint's chapel.

63 · WALL-ARCADING OF THE NORTH CLOISTER WALK · This walk was rebuilt and vaulted in the fourteenth century, the springers remaining in position.

65 · UPPER STAGE OF DUKE HUMPHREY'S CHAPEL · The three tiers of niches on the south front contain seventeen figures of kings.

66 · INTERIOR OF THE RAMRYGE CHAPEL · The tabernacled niches in the upper stage and above the altar are wonderfully preserved though the figures have gone.

67 · THE GREAT GATEHOUSE FROM THE SOUTH · This large three-storied building to the west of the cathedral was the main entrance to the precincts and was built 1365–8. In the turrets are stairways to the upper floors.

68 · WALL-ARCADING OF THE NORTH CLOISTER WALK · All that remains of the cloisters is the wall-arcading on the south wall of the church, disfigured by the buttresses built by Lord Grimthorpe.

70 · THE MODERN WEST FRONT · Of the new façade built by Lord Grimthorpe only the inner parts of the three porches belong to the mediaeval church.

69 · THE OLD WEST FRONT · Until about seventy years ago the west front was as seen above, with a nine-light Perpendicular window of Abbot Wheathampstead's time. The lateral porches had been walled in.

of S. Albans and of the daughter houses should devote themselves to study, writing, illuminating and binding books rather than to outdoor occupations.

Whilst the monk-historians were poring over their manuscripts, there arose within the abbey precincts a school of painters, illuminators, goldsmiths and metal-workers that flourished for more than a century. The artists and craftsmen, of whom the most distinguished were the Colchester family, came to S. Albans at the invitation of one of the monks and here they settled, executing any work required of them for the furnishing or adornment of the abbey church—a figure of the Virgin Mary, a rood or a reredos, a lectern, tablets of silver-gilt or mural paintings. Master Walter of Colchester, the founder of the S. Albans school of painting, came to the abbey with his brothers, William and Simon, and his nephew Richard in 1200. They were then lay-artists, but Walter and Richard embraced the religious life and the 'incomparable Walter' became sacrist in 1213. His fame as an artist spread, for the monks of Canterbury employed him to make the shrine of S. Thomas Becket.

In 1480 a printing press was set up in the great gatehouse of S. Albans, the earliest book produced being *Rhetorica nova Fratris Laurencii Gulielmi de Soana*. Other books followed, notably *Aristotle's Physics*, the *Chronicles of England*, and in 1486 a treatise entitled *The Gentleman's Recreation*, written by the prioress of Sopwell nunnery, and dealing with hawking, hunting and brass armour.

The monks of S. Albans were never very popular with the townspeople, owing to disputes that were constantly arising about rights of pasturage, the felling of timber and hunting. In 1274 the townsmen came into conflict with the monks concerning the use of the abbey mills, a monopoly they were determined to abolish by setting up handmills of their own. In the disorder that resulted, an awkward situation developed for Abbot Roger de Norton. When the tumult was at its height Queen Eleanor arrived at the abbey gate and the abbot had to smuggle her in by a private way in order to elude the townspeople, clamorous with their grievances. Thus infuriated they barricaded the approaches to the town and seized and executed the constable of

Hertford castle, an outrage that cost them a fine of 100 marks. More alarming were the disturbances of 1327 that followed the abbot's refusal to grant the town a charter of liberties. The monastery was besieged but the king intervened and a Court of Arbitration patched up peace for a while.

During the Peasants' Revolt of 1381 an attack was made on the abbey by Wat Tyler's adherents who broke through the great gatehouse, set free the prisoners there and forced their way into the cloisters. To appease the rebels Abbot de la Mare surrendered the charters he held depriving the town of its liberties; but fortunately for the convent the death of Wat Tyler and the arrest of the ringleaders put an end to the rising.

The peace of the monastery was again disturbed during the Wars of the Roses. After the first battle of S. Albans in 1455, though the town was looted by the Yorkist followers the abbey was spared; but it did not emerge unscathed from the disorders that followed the second battle of S. Albans in 1461. The victorious Lancastrians ran amok in the town and despite a royal proclamation, they raided the abbey granaries, storehouses and cellars. Queen Margaret, 'she-wolf of France', helped herself to a jewel from the monastic treasury. So desperate was the plight of the monks that a number of the faint-hearted fled with the abbot to Wheathampstead.

THE LAST DAYS OF THE MONASTERY

In 1536 when Thomas Cromwell, the Vicar-General, appointed commissioners to undertake visitations of all the religious houses in the land, John ap Rice, an unscrupulous knave, was despatched to S. Albans abbey. He reported that he 'found little, although there was much to be found'. Acting upon the Commissioners' findings, Henry VIII induced Parliament to pass an Act to dissolve the lesser monasteries, i.e. those whose income did not exceed £200 a year. For a time the monks of S. Albans breathed freely, but though their house was one of 'the great and solemn monasteries for which Parliament thanked God' and escaped the net of confiscation, they can have been under no delusions. On 10 December 1537 Cromwell's emissaries were again at S. Albans, and the uncompromising attitude of Abbot Robert Catton, 1530–8, made their task a far from easy one. 'In all communications or motions made concerning any surrender [of the abbey] he showeth himself so stiff that as he saith, he will choose to beg his bread all the days of his life than consent to surrender.' Deaf to all persuasion, Abbot Catton remained steadfast and the visitors reported 'he waxeth hourly more obstinate and less conformable'. Obstinate abbots were to be got rid of. Catton was deprived and replaced by Robert Boreman, a willing tool whom Cromwell had made prior of S. Albans a few months before.

When a second Act was procured to suppress all the religious houses, Abbot Boreman signed the deed on 5 December 1539 that surrendered the church, the abbey buildings and all the possessions of the monastery to his royal master. The brethren then numbered thirty-eight, including the prior, and there were also numerous lay servants attached to the abbey, workers in the kitchen and pantry, bakers and brewers, tailors and launderers, porters and stablemen. Abbot Boreman was awarded a pension of £266. 13s. 4d., equal to £10,000 of our money, and the monks having voluntarily surrendered received annuities. Just before the Suppression the annual revenue of the house amounted to £2,102 7s. 1¾d., a very large sum indeed.

In February 1540 the cloisters and all the conventual buildings except the Great Gatehouse were granted by the king to Sir Richard Lee who almost at once cleared the site, so that very little now remains. It is however possible from documentary evidence to make a paper reconstruction of the monastic buildings as they existed in the sixteenth century.

THE CLOISTRAL BUILDINGS

The precincts of the abbey were enclosed by walls and were entered by several gateways of which only the Great Gatehouse to the west of the cathedral is now standing. At the north-east was the Waxhouse Gate where were made the innumerable candles that were burned on the altars and before the images and shrines in the church. On the site of 'The Fighting Cocks' at the south-west and close to the monastic granary was S. Germain's Gate and

in the south-east corner of the precincts stood Holy Well Gate.

The Great Gatehouse, erected by Abbot de la Mare, c. 1365–8, is a large three-storied building, Perpendicular Gothic in style, with a wide archway, battlemented parapets and turret-stairways. The archway and the adjoining chambers are vaulted in stone and below the ground level are a number of cellars which may have been dungeons, for both before the Dissolution and since, the gatehouse was used as a prison.

Within the precincts and mostly south of the abbey church were the various monastic buildings, the infirmary, the lodgings of the abbot and prior, the guest-house, granary, brew-house and stables and all that were necessary for the self-contained life of the monks and for purposes of hospitality.

The buildings occupied by the monks were grouped about the cloisters to the south of the abbey nave. Around a square stretch of lawn covered walks gave access to all the apartments, and were the resort of the brethren during the hours that were set aside for meditation and study. On the wall of the church are the remains of the fourteenth-century arcading of the north cloister-walk, and the west and south walks are still to be traced in the turf. Above the east and south walks Abbot de la Moote built a library and scriptorium, c. 1398.

During the thirteenth and fourteenth centuries so many alterations were made in buildings ranged round the cloisters that few if any of the Norman period were standing at the time of the Suppression.

On the east side of the cloisters was a two-storied block comprising the chapter-house, the dorter or monks' dormitory and the rere-dorter or necessarium. In the chapter-house, a rectangular apartment rebuilt by Abbot Wheathampstead, the monks assembled every morning before High Mass to conduct the business and everything concerning the administration of the house; the abbot occupied a raised seat at the east end with his officers or obedientiaries on either side. Between the chapter-house and the south transept of the church was a slype, a passage that led to the monks' cemetery, south of the choir. Beneath the dorter was the calefactorium or warming-house whither the brethren resorted on cold winter days to warm themselves at a fire for a brief hour or so. The calefactorium was probably used as the day-room in the summer.

Projecting eastwards from the dorter range was the chapel of S. Cuthbert, built by Abbot Daubeney (p. 22) and reconstructed by Abbot Trumpington.

The chief building to the south of the cloisters was the frater or refectory, at each end of which was a passage leading to a quadrangle that was probably the Kitchen Court. On its western side stood the kitchen buildings which conveniently served the monks' frater and another dining-hall known as the Oriole on the south side of the court. The Oriole was used by monk-guests and was also a flesh-frater where on occasion certain of the brethren were permitted to eat meat. It is first mentioned during the rule of Abbot Michael de Mentmore, 1335–41.

The western range of the cloistral buildings known as the cellarium was two stories in height. On the ground floor in proximity to the kitchen were the cellarer's storerooms and at the northern end, built against the wall of the abbey church was the abbot's chapel. The upper floor was used as a guest-house. To the west of the cellarium was a courtyard with the abbot's lodging on the north and bounded on the west by a large guest-hall.

East of the main cloistral buildings lay the Farmery or monks' infirmary consisting of a hall with a chapel at the east, as at Canterbury and Ely, a small cloister and a garden; and north of the farmery was the lodging of the second-in-command, the prior.

Such in brief was the arrangement of the conventual buildings of the premier Benedictine abbey in England, the habitation of men who voluntarily shut themselves away from the world to devote their lives to the monastic obligations of unceasing prayer, hospitality and almsgiving.

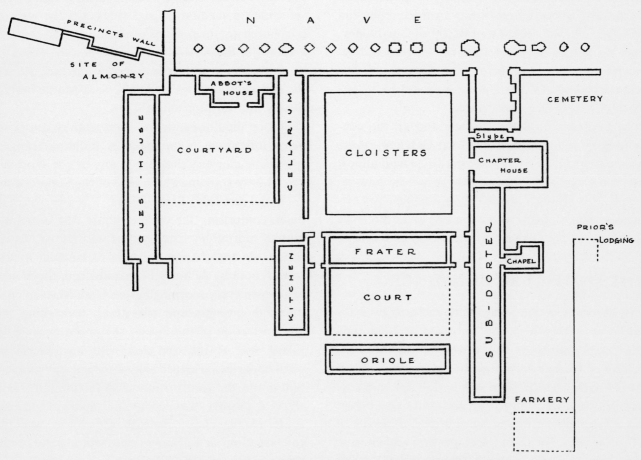

FIG. III. PLAN OF CLOISTRAL BUILDINGS [DESTROYED]

61

Appendix A

Paintings on the Nave Piers

The paintings on the Norman piers were revealed about eighty years ago when the Reformation white-wash was cleaned off. The subjects depicted on the western faces can be identified without difficulty, but those on the fronts of the piers are very indistinct. The predominant colour of the paintings is now a reddish-brown.

Commencing at the second pier west of the rood-screen the subjects from east to west are as follows:

FIRST PIER
W. face: A draped figure of Christ crucified. The Coronation of the Virgin.

SECOND PIER
W. face: The Crucifixion. The Annunciation.
S. face: Edward the Confessor and the pilgrim.

THIRD PIER
W. face: The Crucifixion. The Annunciation.
S. face: S. Osyth (?)

FOURTH PIER
W. face: The Crucifixion. The Virgin Mary and Babe.
S. face: S. Thomas Becket.

FIFTH PIER
W. face: A crowned figure of Christ crucified. The Madonna.
S. face: S. Christopher bearing the child Christ.

Appendix B

The Phases of Mediaeval Architecture

English architecture from the Conquest to the Reformation is divided into three periods or phases of development: Norman, Transitional, and Gothic. The Norman period lasted from *c.* 1070 to *c.* 1145 and was followed by Transitional work in which the change was effected from the round-arched style to the pointed Gothic. By about 1190 the pointed arch was in general use in all parts of the country and this led to the development of the Gothic style which obtained for three and a half centuries or more.

The most convenient subdivision of Gothic is based on the treatment of the windows in each century. Thirteenth-century Gothic is known as Early English and embraces fifty years of so-called Lancet work (1200–50) and half a century of Geometrical.

The name Lancet is given to the long narrow windows with acutely pointed heads, and Geometrical to the forms of tracery that fill the upper parts of the windows of the period.

Fourteenth-century Gothic is known as Decorated or Curvilinear, the window tracery assuming curvilinear or flowing forms; and the Gothic of the fifteenth century is termed Perpendicular or Rectilinear and is characterized by the emphasis of the vertical line. Window tracery of this period becomes stiff and rigid. The final phase, that of the sixteenth century, often spoken of as Tudor Gothic, is a late version of Perpendicular.

These subdivisions, however, are very general, nor was progress the same in all parts of the country. The second half of each century should be regarded as a transitional period, in which new forms were being evolved which became characteristic of the Gothic of the succeeding century.

Appendix C

Dimensions of the Cathedral (approximate)

Total length (external)	550 feet
Total length (internal)	520 feet
Superficial area	39,240 sq. feet
Length of nave (internal) . .	275 ft. 6in.
Width of nave and aisles :	
Western end	77 ft. 9 in.
Eastern end	75 feet
Height of nave	66 ft. 4 in.
Height of tower	144 feet
West front (N. to S.) . . .	105 feet
Length of transepts (N. to S.) . .	177 feet
Length of presbytery and Saint's chapel .	92 ft. 4 in.
Length of retrochoir . . .	44 feet
Width of retrochoir . . .	77 feet
Length of Lady Chapel . . .	57 feet
Width of Lady Chapel	24 feet
Height of Lady Chapel	33 feet

Glossary

AMBULATORY. A procession path carried round the east end of the choir of a church.

ANNULET. A ring of stone or metal in which was fixed a length of detached shafting.

APSE. A semicircular termination of a choir, chapel or aisle.

ARCADE. A range of arches springing from piers or columns and carrying a wall.

BALL-FLOWER. A globular flower with incurved petals.

BAY. A compartment which forms the unit of design in the interior of a church. It extends from one pier to the next and in large churches consists of three stages : arcade, triforium and clerestory.

CHEVRON. A zigzag ornament in common use by Norman masons of the twelfth century.

CLERESTORY. The top stage of the wall above a nave or choir arcade.

CROCKET. A carved clump of foliage applied to arches and gables as a means of decoration.

CROSSING. The central area of a cruciform church where nave, choir and transepts meet.

DOG-TOOTH. A small crossed ornament of thirteenth-century Gothic.

FERETRUM. A coffer or chest containing the relics of a saint.

GROINED VAULT. One in which the intersecting of the vault surfaces are not strengthened with ribs.

HOOD-MOULD. A projecting moulding over an arch.

IMPOST. A horizontal projecting member at the springing of an arch.

LANCET WINDOW. A long, narrow window with a pointed arch at its head.

MENSA. The slab or table-top of an altar.

MULLIONS. Vertical stone bars which divide a Gothic window into a number of 'lights'.

PIER. A mass of masonry built up in courses and supporting one or more arches.

PILASTER. A flat rectangular column applied to a wall or a pier.

PLATE TRACERY. The pierced shapes in the spandrels of an arch.

PRESBYTERY. The eastern part of the choir of a great church.

QUADRIPARTITE VAULT. One divided into four cells by intersecting diagonal ribs.

QUATREFOIL. A design of four lobes or foils.

REREDOS. The screen, panelling or painting behind an altar.

RESPOND. A half-pier attached to a wall and carrying an arch.

RETROCHOIR. That part of a church that lies east of the choir and serves as an ambulatory.

RITUAL CHOIR. In monastic churches, two or three bays of the nave where were the monks' stalls.

SANCTUARY. That part of the presbytery adjacent to the High Altar.

SLYPE. A narrow passage.

SOFFIT. The underside of an arch.

SPANDREL. The triangular area of walling above arches.

SPRINGER. The bottom courses of an arch or a vault.

TABERNACLING. Elaborate canopy work above a reredos, tomb or stall.

TIERCERON. An extra rib rising up to the ridge of a vault.

TRACERY. The curved forms in the head of a Gothic window.

TRIFORIUM. The middle stage in the bay design of a church.

VAULT. A stone roof or ceiling.

VAULTING SHAFT. A stone or marble shaft supporting a bracket from which spring the ribs of a vault.

VOUSSOIR. One of the stones composing an arch.

WALL ARCADING. A range of small arches carried by slender shafts applied as decoration to a wall